Praise for *99 THINGS YOU WANT TO KNOW BEFORE STRESSING OUT!*

"This book will literally save lives. As a two-time cancer conquer I'm using it on a daily basis as a part of my de-cancering program. Each page provides practical life-giving steps and strategies that will put you on the path to creating inner peace. Keep it by your bed on the nightstand and read it regularly as I do and you will discover how to live your life from the inside out. I love and admire Lauren and her commitment to teach people how to add life to their years and years to their life." —**Les Brown, World Renowned Speaker, Author**

"Lauren Miller's 99 Things You Want To Know Before Stressing Out! *is a searching analysis of the sources of stress in our lives, as well as a compendium of incredibly useful tools to regain our balance. However, it is so much more. Concepts such as grace, gratefulness, and being truly present in life, are not mere words in this book. Lauren Miller has lived them, sometimes under dire circumstances, and has incorporated them into the fabric of her daily life and its inevitable challenges. Overflowing with wisdom, peppered with telling examples from the front lines of stress, Ms. Miller leads us to a deeper sense of our own God-given glory in this universe. I*

read the compelling Preface, was hooked immediately, and thereafter trusted Lauren Miller to lead me the rest of the way on a journey of grace and fulfillment." —**Jimmy Roberts,** ***composer of the hit Off Broadway musical, I Love You, You're Perfect, Now Change.***

"Lauren E. Miller has created the guidebook everyone should invest in, in order to help them move from stress to calm. The great news is, even if you are not stressed, this is a beautiful reminder of how to embrace remaining calm, grateful and joyful as your enjoyment of life moves to a wonderful exciting level."—**Peggy McColl,** ***New York Times Best Selling Author***

"There's a six letter word that is an emotional curse. It wreaks havoc on our health—both mentally and physically. That word is STRESS. Author Lauren Miller had more reasons than most to suffer from this affliction. She was in the ring battling breast cancer, 12 surgeries and a divorce —all at the same time. And she came out as a victor not a victim. Share her experience in learning how to overcome stress. I don't know a woman or man who wouldn't benefit from this book." —**Ellen Levine,** ***Editorial Director, Heart Magazines***

"If you read and apply the wisdom found in <u>99 Things You Want to Know Before Stressing Out!</u> then stress will no longer have its way with you.

In addition to powerful stress relief tips, Lauren reminds the reader of life's simple truths that lead to instant peace that we often forget along the way. The insights found in this book have the potential of transforming your entire perception of life along with your response to it." — **Jill Lublin,** ***Best Selling Author/ International Speaker***

"Everyone experiences stress but these days; high levels seem to be an ordinary part of life. Lauren gives her readers a path to reduce stress by providing specific tools they can deploy to improve their lives and achieve the peace all of us crave. Lauren uses her own deeply personal and extraordinary experiences for each reader's benefit. Her inspirational life and commitment to helping all of us radiate throughout this book. The result is a unique and tested tool set anyone can use to significantly improve his or her life."
—Aaron Harber, ***On-Air Host & Executive Producer, USATALK NETWORK, The Aaron Harber Show***

99 Things You Want to Know Before Stressing Out!

Your personal guide back to inner peace & life satisfaction

Lauren E Miller, M.Ed

EDGE GOD IN PRESS

Published by
Published by Edge God In Press
www.EdgeGodIn.com

© 2017, Lauren E Miller, M.Ed
All rights reserved. No part of this book may be reproduced in any form or by any electronic or mechanical means, including information storage and retrieval systems, without permission in writing from the publisher, except by a reviewer who may quote brief passages in a review.

The author has done his/her best to present accurate and up-to-date information in this book, but he/she cannot guarantee that the information is correct or will suit your particular situation.

This book is sold with the understanding that the publisher and the author are not engaged in rendering any legal, accounting or any other professional services. If expert assistance is required, the services of a competent professional should be sought.

All scripture references come from: The Thompson Chain-Reference® Bible New International Version, Copyright© 1983 by The B.B. Kirkbride Bible company, Inc. and The Zondervan Corporation. Used by permission. All rights reserved.

Cover design and Layout by
DocUmeantDesigns
www.DocUmeantDesigns.com

Copy Editor
Karen Kaufman Gauthier

For inquiries about volume orders, please contact:
Lauren E Miller at info@LaurenEMiller.com

LCCN: 2015942114

Printed in the United States Of America
ISBN-13: 978-0999417249   (paperback)

DEDICATION

To my husband: A beautiful rainbow at the end of the storm . . . you are an angel in an Earth suit! And to my three children: Kaylin . . . you embody true love, wisdom and light from God; Johnny . . . your insights, sense of humor and gift of laughter brighten my world; Kimberly . . . your sensitivity and thoughtfulness are God's hands and heart in our home.

Every day I am filled with gratitude for the opportunity you all give me to learn how to love better and let go in this world!

Contents

Dedication iii
Preface xi
Acknowledgments xv
Chapter 1: To Stress? or Not To Stress? . . 1
  #1: Know Stress; Know Dis-ease . . . No Stress;
      No Dis-ease 2
  #2: Gratitude Can Save Your Life. 3
  #3: Staying Sane in the Midst of
      Insanity. 4
  #4: Careful What You Think: Your Body
      Is Listening. 6
  #5: Why is This Happening?!? 7
  #6: Tips to Release Family Anxiety 8
  #7: Jumpstart Your Morning!. 10
  #8: Whatever You Focus on Grows
      Bigger 11
  #9: Use Your Delete Key in Life 12
Chapter 2: You're Not Your Hair, Breasts
or Muscles 15
  #10: I See You As I Am 15
  #11: Mirrors Distort the True You. 17
  #12: Remember You 18
  #13: Guard Your Heart 19
  #14: Get Off Your Emotional Roller
       Coaster 20
  #15: What's Wrong with Me? 22
  #16: You Before the False Beliefs 23
  #17: The Disease to Please 24

#18: Whose Voice is Behind Your
   Self-Image?..................... 25

Chapter 3: The Brush of Death is the Kiss of Life.........................27

#19: Don't Die with The Music Still
   in You!....................... 27
#20: Take Back Your Ability to Heal ... 29
#21: Laughter Can Save Your Life 30
#22: Respect through Suffering 31
#23: Loss Leads to Perspective........ 32
#24: Possibilities from Pain 33
#25: Remove Your Mask of Pain 35
#26: Life's Chutes and Ladders® 36
#27: Visit a Graveyard............... 37

Chapter 4: I'm Ok, You're Ok ... I'm Not Ok, You're Not Ok 39

#28: Self Esteem: Belief in Oneself 39
#29: Know Your Body's 'YES' and 'NO' 41
#30: Belief in YOU Solves Workplace
   Anxiety...................... 42
#31: Stay in Your Castle 44
#32: Collaboration Over Competition . 45
#33: Release Leads to Peace 47
#34: Remember Your Worth!......... 48
#35: Shift Your Focus: Shift Your Life .. 49
#36: Personal Peace Process.......... 50

Chapter 5: Did You Know You're An Addict?...........................53

#37: The Drug of Approval........... 53
#38: Stuck in Your Attachments?...... 54
#39: Who Wrote on Your Wall?....... 55

#40: The Prison of: What Will Other People Think? 56
#41: Are You a "Take Everything Personally" Addict? 57
#42: It's Not Rejection, It's Just Direction 58
#43: The "I'll Get to It Tomorrow" Rut   59
#44: Simplify and Organize Your Life. . 60
#45: The Lying Addiction: It's More Common than You Think 61

Chapter 6: The Boat or Jesus 63
#46: Practice Living Life 63
#47: Failure is a Perspective 65
#48: You Can Walk on Top of Water . . . 66
#49: Living Outside Your Boat. 67
#50: Stop the Craze of Addictions and Cravings 69
#51: Resurrect Your Voice 71
#52: Are You Addicted to Your Trauma? 72
#53: Clean Out Your Matrix. 73
#54: I Have To Be Perfect . . . OR ELSE! 74

Chapter 7: These Two Commandments Can Transform Your Life. 77
#55: You Give What You Want. 77
#56: Who Would You Be Without Your Wounds? 79
#57: Success Is Not a Secret 80
#58: Peace: Consistent Sincerity and Reverence for All of Life. 81
#59: Life Is To Love and To Be Loved . . 81
#60: Move from the King of Your Organs 82
#61: Love Exists Outside of Desire 84
#62: Choose Love. 84

#63: Dance, Whistle, Sing............ 85

Chapter 8: To Be? Or Not To Be?...... 87
#64: Observe versus React to Life 87
#65: Who Do I Say Sent Me? 88
#66: Begin Again 89
#67: Be Still and Know 90
#68: How Do I Do This?............. 91
#69: Random Acts of Kindness 93
#70: Understanding Omnipresence ... 94
#71: Linger in Life 95
#72: Are You Defined By Your List? ... 95

Chapter 9: Remain Open to Love...... 97
#73: You Always Do That! 97
#74: You Don't Love Me 98
#75: The Distortion Dilemma 99
#76: Emotions Block Me from Seeing You 100
#77: I Love You Because You Love Me 101
#78: The Guilt Factor............... 102
#79: The Jealousy Jungle 103
#80: Own, Control and Possess 104
#81: Giving Your Power Away 105

Chapter 10: Do You Bend or Break? .. 107
#82: The Rainbow in The Midst of the Storm 107
#83: Goals, Deadlines and Appointments 109
#84: Something Inside You is Superior to Circumstance................ 110
#85: Complaining IS a Choice 111
#86: The Sky Remains Blue beyond the Clouds....................... 111

#87: God's Love is a Constant 112
#88: Avoid the Deer in the Headlights 113
#89: Just Let It Go!. 114
#90: Do You Fight, Fly, or Freeze?. . . . 116

Chapter 11: Is Your Anchor Sinking Your Boat?. 119

#91: Expectations and Assumptions Sink Your Boat 119
#92: Curiosity and Fascination Float Your Boat 120
#93: Go With the Flow 121
#94: Avoid Tunnel Vision: Expand Your Options. 122
#95: Practice Integrity. 123
#96: EGO Sinks: Vulnerability Floats . 124
#97: Look for the Lighthouse. 125
#98: Love People, Not Things. 126
#99: Don't Want to Sink? Learn How to Swim. 127

Bonus Chapter: Getting Your Energy Behind the Shift 129

About the Author 137

Preface

Four years ago I was diagnosed with advanced breast cancer and told I had a 50 percent chance of survival one week prior to my final divorce court date. My business was, and is, empowering people worldwide to live life without stress. So, here I was facing two of the top stressors in life. WOW! What an amazing schoolhouse of opportunity to practice what I had been learning and teaching for 18 years!

In less than two years I experienced a divorce, a double mastectomy, 12 surgeries, 16 rounds of chemo, one year of Herceptin® infusions, six weeks of daily radiation and a blood staph infection. I have no feelings of victimization in any of this because it truly led to an amazing connection with all of humanity . . . we all have our "dark night of the soul" experiences and how we choose to respond to them makes ALL the difference in the outcome!

So what did I learn? I'm not my breasts. I'm not my hair. When I connect to my breath, I connect to the present moment and when I am present the grace I need to handle ANY situation shows up every time. At any moment I can choose to connect to inner peace. I learned how to be a fascinated, curious human being vs. one who is imprisoned by assumptions and attachments. Victimization keeps you in a state of emotional paralysis. Asking "how" questions vs. "why" questions leads to creative solutions. I cannot be grateful and depressed at the same time. Whatever I choose to focus on GROWS BIGGER quickly! I learned how to accept all of my emotions without judgment. I learned that when you are graced with the brush of death, you are given the gift of instant perspective of all that is truly essential in this life. Ultimately, I learned that I am a drop of life in God's endless ocean of possibilities . . . ALL things are possible for me . . . and you.

"Nothing thrives in a state of war" is a powerful lesson that I learned in the midst of the battle for my life. Here is a little flash from my past that played a part in this life lesson:

I found myself standing in a ring at the Tae Kwon Do State Championships, facing my opponent—who happened to be 10 years younger than me. The bell went off and the punching and kicking began. All of a sudden, everything went black as I found myself lying flat on my back listening to the drone of a countdown . . . 10 . . . 9 . . . 8 . . . 7 . . . 6 . . . 5 . . . 4 . . . "Wait a minute" a voice within me shouted, "I didn't train four hours a day, six days a week for an entire year to go out like this . . . get up Lauren! GET UP, GET UP!"

All of a sudden, a surge of strength coursed through my being, pushing me up to my feet. I stood eye to eye with my attacker who had done two illegal moves that landed her foot on the side of my head. The bell rang again and this time I had so much anger coursing through me that I lost touch with my 8th degree black belt Master. He was shouting from the sidelines in a desperate attempt to ground me enough so I could connect to my skills and techniques. Whenever there is a powerful emotion in life, positive or negative, you cannot see clearly or respond with wisdom. I ended up looking like I was lost in the forest at birth and raised by a bunch of wild monkeys . . . anger and frustration fueled every kick and punch. I ended up winning that round . . . but really? I forgot everything my Master had taught me in the heat of my emotions.

From his perspective, I didn't win using the art I was trained in. Rather, I fought like a wild spider monkey and clawed my way to the silver medal.

In Tae Kwon Do you learn very small aspects of movement and mental focus before breaking 15 boards and stepping into a State Championship ring. The training is intense and seems endless at times. Yet when practiced with wisdom, it has the potential to save your life.

Ten years later, once again, everything went black, and I found myself flat on my back; bald and breastless. Replacing the countdown I heard in the ring were the voices of doctors and nurses calling out "Code Blue! Code Blue!" Rather than anger, I felt the most profound peace and safety—as if I was floating above all pain, worry, doubt and fear. Yet, I was very much aware of the distress in the lives of those clamoring around me as they attempted to pull me back from a heart malfunction. Rather than being fueled by anger like the first time I was knocked out, I was fueled by the choice for love and life no matter what surrounded me.

This was the first "kiss of death" I experienced in a two-year period of time. Each "brush of death" experience delivered the same profound peace, release and instant perspective; validating a curiosity that I had spent my life exploring: "Is it possible to remain in a place of love and peace no matter what surrounds you?" I stand in awe of how quickly my entire perception shifts to peace and safety as soon as all the paralyzing fears get out of the way. St. Augustine spoke to this experience when he said he found great peace whenever he gave his spirit permission to guide his flesh into all things. As soon as my *flesh* got out of the way during my "kiss of death" experiences, my spirit took over and peace returned.

The intention of this book is to provide you with small pieces of information that perhaps you once knew and simply forgot. When rediscovered and nurtured daily, these pieces of information hold within themselves the potential to move mountains and maintain inner peace.

Stress is simply a signal within your body offering you the opportunity to identify and adjust your perception of any situation. My hope is that within these pages you will find a treasure box of essential tips, reminders and tools that will empower you to shift into peace in the midst of any challenging situation as well as expand your experience of life satisfaction and sustainable joy.

Visit LaurenEMiller.com for your FREE bonus Stress Relief Video Gift.

Acknowledgments

To my God, parents, family and friends who continually remind me of what I value most in life. Thank you for the opportunities you give me daily to learn how to release the non-essentials in my day and to pursue love and connection, which is the only experience in life that holds within itself value that lasts beyond my next breath and heartbeat.

TO STRESS? OR NOT TO STRESS?

Ahhh . . . that is the question. Did you know you have the ability to choose your response to any and every situation that unfolds before you in life? When you remember this truth, it is very empowering and will be of great worth as you journey through life. Your choice of response will also make all the difference in the outcome. When you choose any strong emotional response, know that you cannot see things for what they really are because you are blinded by the intensity of the emotion. You might say, "Well, I can't help myself, that's just how I respond," which comes from your subconscious patterns of behavior. However, when you become conscious of behaviors and responses that no longer serve you, you are in a position to shift back to peace. To choose to stress or not to stress, the choice is yours. Simply taking a few deeps breaths between the situation and your response to it can give you a little gap of empowerment to choose peace over panic.

#1: Know Stress; Know Dis-ease . . . No Stress; No Dis-ease

A recent study out of UCLA's Jonsson Comprehensive Cancer Center revealed that chronic stress acts as a sort of fertilizer to cancer cells. If you know anything about the physiological effects of stress on the body from high blood pressure to increased cortisol levels and a compromised immune system you might say, "You think?" At least that's what I said when I read the findings.

It was one week prior to my final divorce court date when I was diagnosed with stage-three breast cancer. Because I don't believe in divorce (in *my tribe* you stay married for life) I was under some serious stress and my body was talking to me about it all. Have you ever broken down the word disease? Dis-ease: Feelings of uneasiness in the body due to perceived situations that are seen by the viewer as a potential threat to their safety (emotionally, physically or spiritually).

Two of your core needs in life are connection and safety. When you feel unsafe you feel disconnected and you begin to stress out: "Oh no, I'm not safe; I might fail; I might be fired; I might be unseen, unheard, or overlooked." One way to disconnect from feelings of insecurity is to connect to that which *is* secure within you—along with what you value most in life. What do you value most in your life? I would venture to guess that it exists beyond the five senses. Make a list of everything that you value most in this life and take time every day to nurture one or two things on that list. You will find that when you align yourself to that which you value most, you fertilize your sense of safety in all situations. This, in turn, releases a sense of ease in your body. Surely, a portion of the time you spend Skyping, texting, emailing and cell phoning can be used to create ease in your daily life, especially knowing it has the potential to save your life. When your priorities are clear your decisions are easy, which in turn lowers the stress and dis-ease level inside of your body. Remember, it's your choice. One of my daily mantras is "people before things." Each time I practice this throughout the day I am given the opportunity to choose between the essential and the nonessential. When you connect with the essential, the result is a life of value and inner peace. As Dr. David Hawkins points out, *"Peace is the natural state when truth prevails."* Align yourself with truth, what is good, pure, excellent and praiseworthy.

#2: Gratitude Can Save Your Life

Yes, it's true that when you practice random acts of kindness and gratitude on a daily basis you get physiological benefits in the Earth suit:

- Increased immune system
- Improved cognitive performance
- Increased energy
- Lower heart rate
- Balanced cortisol (hydrocortisone) levels, which result in less internal stress

- More likely to live a longer and a more satisfied life
- Laughter and inner joy resulting in decreased stress hormones
- Lower blood pressure and
- Diminished pain

Wow, that's a lot of benefits! So, how often throughout your day do you practice gratitude and carry out random acts of kindness to those around you, including yourself?

When the cloud of depression appeared in the midst of my chemo treatments, I remember experimenting with different techniques to see which one was the quickest at removing the clouds. Gratitude won me over every time. You cannot be depressed and grateful at the same time. Talk about a destructive cloud in life to remove. Whenever I shifted my focus from the "stressful situation" of the divorce, chemo, radiation and surgery to all that I was grateful for—down to my very heartbeat—the darkness lifted instantly. Try it. The next time you're feeling down and out, do a random act of kindness to yourself. Start reviewing all that you are grateful for in life. Wake up to all the wondrous ways God will come to you today, perhaps in a smile, an open door, a moment in nature, or a song.

#3: Staying Sane in the Midst of Insanity

According to a recent study by the American Psychological Association, 75% of Americans experience "mega stress."

To Stress? or Not To Stress?

Stress is simply a signal within your body giving you an amazing opportunity to identify and adjust your perception of a situation, along with your behavior. We forget that whatever we focus on grows bigger quickly . . . positive or negative. Here are three quick tips to help you stay sane in the midst of the insanity:

- This is worth repeating: **know what you value most in life.** Stress creeps in when you forget what you value most in life. When you spend most of your energy on the "non-essentials" in life, you begin to feel depleted very quickly, and the stress hormone begins to double. Create moments, every day, which nurture what you value most in this life and notice how quickly clarity of thinking and inner peace return.

- **Let go of this belief: In order to be loved and accepted, I need to be perfect . . . have** the perfect house, relationship, car, person, family, job, credentials. What is your inner list of requirements in order to feel loved and accepted in life? Let go of your need for certain outcomes in order for you to feel good about yourself. Happiness returns when you release the attachments you have in life in order to feel good about you. Remember, joy flows from the inside out, not the outside in. Start loving yourself completely—just as you are, right where you are. If you lack it, borrow it from God's heart, where the supply is limitless.

- **Breathe, Breathe, Breathe** . . . and be present to the 'Silent, Holy Night' that dwells within every moment of life. Give yourself the gift of empowerment that comes when you become the observer of your life versus the reactor. Be a curious and fascinated human being who looks at everything before them as an opportunity for learning and growth. When one door closes, don't waste one moment looking at that closed door, start seeking the open window. Don't miss life. When you have worry, doubt and fear, you miss the life standing right in front of your face. When you are present, you will laugh more. Laughter has profound physiological benefits; yet another wonderful gift to give yourself and those around you.

#4: Careful What You Think: Your Body Is Listening

You are the gatekeeper for your thoughts, positive or negative. You get to choose what you keep and what you release. *"Whether you believe you can or you can't, you're right!"* —Henry Ford. As you believe, so shall it be! Jesus often explored the belief of the one who was to be healed before the healing occurred. The miracles took place according to the faith of those receiving them. Belief is essential for any lasting transformation in this life to take place. Your thoughts flow from your beliefs and many of those beliefs manifested out of negative situations in life: I'm unworthy, unlovable, incapable; nothing ever works out for me; for anything to be worthwhile it needs to be difficult; I'm a loser; and on and on.

The water studies from Japan came to my awareness during my experience with cancer. The impact visually inspired me to make it a practice to watch the words I used throughout my treatment and subsequent healing. Basically, our bodies are made up of 70% water. Dr. Masaru Emoto, author of *The Hidden Messages in Water*, discovered that crystals formed in frozen water reveal changes when specific, concentrated thoughts are directed toward them. He found that water from clear springs (and water exposed to loving words) shows brilliant, complex, and colorful snowflake patterns. In contrast, polluted water (water exposed to negative words) forms incomplete, asymmetrical patterns with dull colors and dark holes. To me, this speaks of the POWER of positive words all the way down to the cellular level!

As Einstein said, *"The field directly affects the particle."* Again, when you connect to what is truly essential in life, loving and being loved, your inner voice will reflect that connection and your body will listen.

"The mind controlled by the Spirit is life and peace" (Romans 8:6).

#5: Why is This Happening?!?
This can be criticism, rejection, grief, loss, pain, illness, family issues, money problems or any other situation that would evoke the response: WHY is this happening? I encourage you to remove this wondering from your life experience because of its ability to keep you in a state

of emotional paralysis. Inspiration and a sense of purpose flow from the experience of letting go of your need to know why things happen as they do. Resisting *what is* in life sets the body up for tension and anxiety. When you release this resistance an abundance of creativity is birthed in the soul.

When you interact with other human beings in this world, take full responsibility for your responses. No human being has the power to make you feel anything, unless you give that power to them. You will often stay stuck repeating negative comments from other people in your head to the point that you miss the opportunities for learning and living right in front of your face. Let go of your need to know why people do what they do or say what they say.

Ask how, when or what questions instead of why questions: How can I return to a place of inner peace? What benefits do I get holding on to this problem? How will I know it is solved? When was a time that this problem was not a problem for me? When you connect yourself to the benefits of solution-based thinking, you are free to learn and grow. When you hold onto your need to know why things happen as they do, you will stay stuck in justifications and reasons without changing anything. Ask yourself solution-focused questions throughout your day and watch how the doors open.

#6: Tips to Release Family Anxiety
Much of your anxiety in family relationships flows from your inner list of requirements that connect you to your '*tribe*'. You connect with the

tribe when you follow the tribal rules, many of which are unspoken. When you feel that you fall short of connecting to your tribe and honoring the tribal codes, anxiety begins to quickly grow. Perhaps it is as simple as when your family gathers for Sunday dinner and one Sunday night you have plans. A common emotional response may be guilt—and all participants have their role in it.

Guilt is a tribal tool that many families use to control their members . . . watch out for it because it serves no one and when you allow yourself to react to it, you become an enabler to this unhealthy behavior. When you give yourself permission to move in a different direction than your *tribe*, you may experience protest. However, when you choose to be a seeker of truth within and around you, peace will eventually return—and in most cases with the tribe members as well.

Remember, whatever a member of your family says or does is not a personal attack on you, unless you *choose* to make it so. Let go of your need to own, control and possess the responses of your family members. Work on feeling that you are sufficient just as you are. Most of your tense relationships flow from your own inner feelings of inadequacy. What if you knew that you already *made it* in life? How would that play out in your family connections? Imagine feeling completely secure just as you are as you relate to those around you. How would your world shift? Explore this concept.

#7: Jumpstart Your Morning!

Ask yourself this question tomorrow morning . . . "Self, what would be a fun creative way to exercise this beautiful body of mine this morning? What works with where I am today?" See what comes up and move in the direction of that energy. Some mornings it may involve pushing all the furniture back and dancing. Other days you may feel like running up and down the stairs and around the house while listening to your favorite music. While yet other times you may want to punch or kick something. The key is to get out of your box. Stretch your view of what exercise needs to look like in order for it to count. There are many ways to move and exercise your 'Earth suit'.

Gratitude is another essential ingredient to use when you jump-start your morning. List three things you are grateful for and three things you are looking forward to in your day. Prayer is a powerful way to start any day of life: "I'm alive today! Thank you God, for another day of life and the opportunity to learn how to love better; including myself. Thank you that I can get up and take care of this healthy body of mine and explore life in so many beautiful ways. Grant me the grace of wonderment in all that I experience today."

Another quick tip: start at your ankles and lightly pat up each leg, your torso, your arms, up the center of your torso, tap your fingers on your chin below your lips, under your nose and end with tapping on the top of your head. Breathe out all the way and relax as you take in a deep breath. You can repeat this a few times to turn on all of your circuit breakers and jump-start your day!

#8: Whatever You Focus on Grows Bigger

Have you ever noticed when you are interested in something like a certain car, a piece of clothing or a specific goal that you tune into it everywhere? This is because of your Reticular Activating System (RAS), the part of your brain located in the brainstem that controls many important functions, including breathing, heartbeats and tuning into what you really want in life. It pulls information from the background noise of life that is congruent with the messages it receives from your conscious mind. For example, if you are in a packed restaurant waiting for your name to be called, your RAS will block out the background noise and help you to tune into your name. Whatever you focus on in life grows bigger, be it positive or negative. The RAS aligns itself with what you believe about yourself: your capabilities and feelings of inadequacy. It is the physiological element behind Henry Ford's statement: *"Whether you believe you can, or you can't, you're right."*

Once you choose your focus, be very specific and release the self-doubt. Even if you shift your wording from: "I can't do this," to "I don't know how yet, and I am willing to trust that I am capable of gathering the information I need to enable me to do this easily," you are shifting enough to activate your RAS and get it working for you rather than against you. Be very specific with your focus. Choose to reframe or erase and replace any goal that is not worded in the positive. It is important to do this because the RAS will believe whatever you focus on: "I can do all things with God," or "I can't do anything right." The evidence to back up what you focus on will start showing up in your life, thanks to your RAS; so choose your focus wisely.

#9: Use Your Delete Key in Life
In light of the previous entry, know that, in your life, you choose your areas of focus. You have the ability to delete what no longer serves you; because of your connection to the familiar, you simply forget that you can do so.

Human beings gravitate toward that which is familiar in life simply because they feel safe, regardless of the effect it has on their overall well-being. "If it's familiar, it's safe." Remember that one of your core needs is safety. With that said, you forget that you can choose to feel safe with the unfamiliar, especially when the unfamiliar is a greater benefit to your inner sense of peace and connection. Many people stay with old patterns of behavior, including negative thinking, because of this one statement: "Who would I be without this in my life?" Yes, even though it's negative, simply because you have identified yourself with it for so long you have created a false sense of safety in that pattern of negative thinking. "It's just who I am," you say. However, it doesn't have to be! And that is the freeing truth!

Become the observer of this crazy addiction to negative patterns in your life simply because they are familiar to you and choose to make the shift to the positive. Use your delete button any time you are consciously aware of a negative pattern. Say out loud, "I choose to delete this, knowing it holds no value toward my inner peace" or simply say, "DELETE." Your body knows what that word means. Follow up with a positive choice, word, phrase, verse or mantra that reconnects you to your God given strength and ability to choose what is good, right, pure, praise worthy and beautiful in this life.

YOU'RE NOT YOUR HAIR, BREASTS OR MUSCLES

Much of your anxiety flows from that to which you attach your self-image . . . when it's gone, for whatever reason, you start to spiral into insecurity.

I didn't think I was attached to my hair and breasts until they were gone. This gave me a profound opportunity to reconnect to the truth of who I am apart from anything outside of me. What a relief to remember that I am not my hair, breasts, eye brows, eye lashes, the cancer or the divorce . . . none of these things define me. Remembering this unleashed a sense of inner freedom to be me that has transformed my daily life.

#10: I See You As I Am
One of my favorite spiritual mentors in life is the Christian mystic Anthony de Mello. He speaks

of the blindness we experience as human beings when it comes to our inability to see each other as we truly are.

This is a message that has been referred to throughout history by many spiritual leaders. Jesus invited us to love our neighbor . . . as ourselves. You can only love those around you, with clear perception, as you love and see yourself. Notice as you go through your day how your entire perception of those around you shifts with your mood. When you are upbeat and happy, you see everyone around you through that lens. When you are upset, down and out, you see everyone through that lens.

Anthony says that having clarity of perception leads to accuracy of response. In other words, when I see me clearly and accept all that I am, just as I am, then I can see you clearly. Perhaps this is what Jesus was referring to when He spoke about removing the plank from your own eye then you can see clearly to remove the speck from your brother's eye. Clarity of perception begins within *you*. What if you could love yourself in the midst of imperfection? How would that affect your view of others? Love evokes love even if it's unseen.

As you remember what you are not, you will gain clarity into the experience of who you are; which in turn will guide your responses to the world around you. You see the world as you see yourself. If you want a shift toward peace, begin within *you* and your entire perception of the world around you will begin to lighten up.

#11: Mirrors Distort the True You
Some cultures believe that the mirror actually robs the soul of its authentic view of self.

After the double mastectomy, I covered my mirrors for one week. I wanted to give myself time to ground my perception of me in God before having any distraction that may cause me to forget who I truly am. I remember the moment those sheets came down. I stood before myself as I surveyed the amputation. I stood bald and breastless, unable to connect to the former physical appearance I had once labeled *"me"*. As my son said, I looked like someone from Star Wars.

In the midst of the removal of my physical appearance, I was given the opportunity to *see me* once again. In an instant, I realized two truths that flowed from the French mystic priest, Teilhard de Chardin: *"I'm acutely aware of my own mortality. So what do you do with that awareness? Love others, love yourself. Have a relationship with God."* Along with: *"We are not human beings having a spiritual experience. We are spiritual beings having a human experience."*

As you remember that you are a spiritual being having a physical experience, you reconnect yourself with aspects of *you* that are not defined by the outer world. You begin to feel an anchor within that protects you from rising and falling depending on how the world judges you in the moment. You resurrect your confidence to live *you* out in the world, and you become fearless.

#12: Remember You

Part of the experience of remembering *who you are,* is knowing what you are not. You are not your physical appearance, past pain, traumas, opinions or the outcomes of situations around you. True inner peace emerges within you when your soul remembers that it has already made it because of its connection to God.

Your subconscious will continue to replay programs from your past, most of which are formed from the time you are born up to six years old. Many of these programs are not representative of who you truly are rather they come from false beliefs about you and past pain. They make up around 95 percent of your responses to the world around you. Isn't that amazing? The majority of your responses to the world flow from these holographs from your past that are the result of you giving power away to someone or some event, and you forget who you truly are.

Simply imagining what your life would be like without some of these false beliefs is enough to put you in the vibration of a new thought pattern. An unknown author once asked, *"What would your life be like if you knew you could not fail?"* What if you believed that you could handle any situation before you and that you would always be okay and safe? Imagine being able to talk to anyone, share your truth in front of any group and ask for what you want in life without any fear, doubt or worry? What would that look like for you? Again, when you fill your wonderings with positive possibilities your brain will tune into those things in your daily life. Humility is a portal through which you pass remembering all that you value most in life. When you remain small in life, humbly grateful for each breath, you are able to connect to all that is larger than life!

Remember what you are NOT, then focus on what you ARE and always have been. You simply forgot because of the past pain and false beliefs. Whatever is forgotten in life has the potential to be remembered. Knowing what, in life, moves you to tears is a good road to travel on when it comes to the experience of remembering you.

#13: Guard Your Heart

Compassion fatigue: when the body becomes physically compromised due to the overwhelming emotions evoked within because of another's pain.

During challenging times, it is essential that you remain acutely aware of your soul and its connection to God. If you allow yourself to entertain thoughts that nurture victimization, you will remain in a state of emotional paralysis: Why did this happen? How could this happen? Hasn't there been enough suffering and pain? AND the ultimate statement: "How could God let this happen?"

All of these statements come from a place within you called the "EGO" which was created by you in order to give you the feeling that you have some sense of control and entitlement to that control. The EGO is based on false self-beliefs that are fed by all that is non-essential in this life.

All truth flows from the soul (often referred to as your heart . . . *follow your heart*). The soul does not need to know why things happen as they do; it exists in connection to the all-knowing God. No matter what happens around you, your soul remains calm and present to all that is essential in this life . . . love and all of its beautiful expressions. Your soul is constantly empowered to take action because it is not preoccupied with needing to know why things happen as they do. It recognizes only what is *real* and moves from a place of truth that has no need to know or understand in order to experience the peace that passes all human understanding.

The soul exists beyond reason: What if? How come? Why me? Why them? Because the soul is not bound or ruled by *thought* it knows no boundaries to creativity and love.

Clarity, vision and purpose are all benefits one experiences when the choice is made, as St. Augustine said, to *"give the soul permission to guide the flesh into all things."* Let us take action from our soul where creativity and love know no limits. Your soul remains untouched and unrestricted by reason.

Knowing that the God of the Universe knows is enough for me to release my need to know why things happen as they do and take faith filled action . . . in love, with love and for love.

#14: Get Off Your Emotional Roller Coaster

Understanding the different factors that lower your emotional threshold can give you the opportunity to nurture those areas in your life and maintain emotional balance and inner peace.

Nurture your emotional state by reevaluating your core beliefs, releasing negative pictures from your past and resolving past trauma. The "Getting Your Energy Behind the Shift" bonus chapter at the end of this book can help you with this. Unforgiveness, fears, doubts and worries along with the inner critic are all factors that lower your emotional threshold and the ability to handle situations in life. Whom do you need to forgive in your life for your own inner healing and peace?

Understand that environmental influences play a major day-to-day part in your emotional stability. We live in a toxic environment, so do your research and make healthy choices every day with your food, water and environment. Be aware of any of the main stressors in life that may be playing a role in your emotional roller coaster: family, work, illness and money. Remember that stress is simply a signal within your body giving you the opportunity to *identify and adjust* your perception of any situation and your behavior. In terms of triggers to your emotional state, be aware of the following: chemicals in food; cosmetics; wheat; inadequate sleep; wireless waves (check out the Q-Link necklace to help with that); dairy; sugar; caffeine; MSG; aspartame; vitamin deficiency. These are actually several of the items you often find on a cancer prevention list.

Don't freak out thinking, "I live in an unsafe world". Use this information to make wise choices in your life; choices that nurture a healthy environment for you. Make one or two adjustments at a time and move in the direction of creating an emotionally balanced *you*.

#15: What's Wrong with Me?
Dr. Bruce Lipton has done some amazing work in this world to prove what Einstein set out to prove: *"The field directly affects the particle."* He says, *"Our beliefs and perception of the environment are the control mechanism that shapes our DNA and health."* WOW, what do you think of that? This is referred to as epigenetics. Dr. Lipton discovered that the environment shapes the development of the cells. He quickly shifted his approach to cellular biology from the belief that the body is a biochemical machine controlled by genes. Therefore, we are victims of our heredity and the medical world will save us to explore the endless possibilities for healing within as a result of shifting our perceptions and beliefs about life. His work is definitely worth exploring.

Your beliefs hold the power to change unhealthy genetic messages into healthy ones. They affect all aspects of your life: your body, fears, memories, goals, possessions, guilt and relationships.

Your negative core beliefs usually have many legs that are holding them up; such as the belief that something is wrong with you. Wrong with you in relation to what? According to whom? What are the aspects behind this belief? Where did you learn that something was wrong with you? How did you come to that conclusion? The problem with your beliefs is that you see them as facts in your life rather than beliefs that can be shifted and adjusted.

Remember, you choose the power you give to your negative beliefs and you can take it back. Even though you believe that something is wrong with you, you can choose to love and accept yourself and move in the direction of healing that harmful belief. Knowing how powerful your beliefs are, down to the cellular level, is enough of a motivation to choose healing. **Heal the belief . . . heal the body.**

Many times you will go back and forth before you finally choose to delete your negative belief: "I'm good enough as I am . . . no I'm not . . . yes I am . . . no I'm not . . . YES, I AM!" Knowing how powerful your beliefs are, down to the cellular level, is enough of a motivation to choose healing. Heal the belief . . . heal the body.

Your life reflects your beliefs, so choose wisely.

#16: You Before the False Beliefs
Your unconscious beliefs about you shape how you see the world around you along with your perception of *you* in the midst of it all.

So the freeing question is: "How do you reconnect to *you* before all of the false beliefs, self-doubts, fears and feelings of un-safety kicked in?"

Begin to tune in on a daily basis to that which moves you in life. As mentioned earlier, when you tune into what moves you to tears you connect to an aspect of you that is authentic in life. What is it? Are you moved by compassionate acts of kindness in life? Beautiful music? Moments of stillness? Beauty in Nature? Connection with those you love? Reminders of what is truly lasting on Earth? Expressions of suffering? Expressions of love? The Arts? Watch yourself carefully and observe what moves you.

Once you discover something, ask yourself a few questions. What is it about this experience that reminds me of myself? Is there something I am moved to explore in my life as a result of seeing this? What part of me is awakened by this experience? How does this reflect something I value in life and how can I nurture that? Is this experience offering me an unexpected opportunity to explore a part of myself that I forgot in the midst of a false belief? Perhaps you love to sing, but your 6th grade teacher said you can't and you believed her, so it became your reality.

Take back your power and redefine yourself in the light of the "all things are possible with God" lens. Start reprogramming your inner computer with programs that reflect you . . . before your false beliefs.

#17: The Disease to Please
The disease to please comes from farming out your sense of identity into the acts of service you do for others. Serving others in this world is a wonderful experience with many emotional and physiological benefits, but you're trapped when your sense of who you are is directly linked to what you do for others. You have given your power away to something or someone outside of *you*; this leaves you vulnerable to emotional instability. The disease to please is often accompanied by this statement: "Who would I be if I was unable to please those around me?"

Perfectionism also walks hand-in-hand with the *disease to please*: "In order to love and accept myself, what I do for others must be done perfectly; at least it must follow my inner criteria for perfection." Often these beliefs are associated with the need to please in order to feel good about yourself: "I'm unseen, unheard, underappreciated, not good enough, incapable, overlooked and invalidated."

A vicious cycle often accompanies this condition: "I please you; then I feel good about me. I don't please you; then I don't feel good about me."

How about exploring what needs to shift in terms of your perception of *you?* Practice feeling good about *yourself*, with or without pleasing those around you. The power of living your life without attaching your sense of self to any experience outside of you is truly exhilarating!

#18: Whose Voice is Behind Your Self-Image?

Next time you feel the cloud of self-doubt rolling in ask yourself: "Whose voice is behind this?"

Remember, you will rise and fall depending on how you perceive the world is judging you as long as you farm out your sense of identity to the world around you. You have been farming yourself out for quite a long time; giving permission to people, circumstances and events to write on your wall (define me).

As soon as you pass your pen to another human being, the belief begins. It's as if you say, Who do you say that I am? Oh, okay then that's what I will believe . . . for the rest of my life." This will continue until you erase it and replace it with a firm belief about yourself that is in line with who you truly are.

Take back your pen and write what you believe to be true in life. Then, next to each belief, write out where you learned it and whose voice is behind it. This is a very helpful exercise when it comes to erasing the messages on your inner wall that no longer serve your well-being and inner peace. Once you have a face, event or circumstance behind your negative belief, it is easier to reframe your sense of self into a positive perception: That was then, this is now, I am willing to consider forgiving, letting go and remembering that who *I am* exists outside of any opinion, trauma or circumstance. I am not the abuse, judgment or painful experience in life. I am created in love, for love and by love, and I choose to remember and embrace that perception of me.

THE BRUSH OF DEATH IS THE KISS OF LIFE

The kiss of life is anything that brings instant perspective along with it concerning all that is truly essential, beautiful and lasting.

#19: Don't Die with The Music Still in You!
As I walked through the experience of cancer and divorce, I got the opportunity to reconnect with all that had become disconnected due to past pain and false beliefs. Part of that reconnect was with the music within me. At 38 I was diagnosed with advanced cancer one week prior to my final divorce court date and given a 50 percent chance of survival. I am a second degree black belt and at that time had a business training women in the areas of emotional, physical and spiritual well-being and inner balance. HOWEVER, when I got that phone call the inner balance went out the door. I threw myself on the ground kicking, cry-

ing, and screaming against the diagnosis. I cried these words out to God, "I still have music to play to the world inside of me . . . bring to me everything I need to heal." I have always connected to music. When I was growing up we had a family band. I played the drums and the piano and my brother and I would put on little musical shows for my family. Music is woven into my being.

Life is a musical . . . a beautiful symphony of love, joy and gratitude all birthed through the experience of pain, loss and suffering (if you choose to see it this way). Each challenge in life is an opportunity to weave a note of love, forgiveness and healing into this melodic song of life. The most captivating truth about this song is that it is meant to be a shared experience. It has no limits, boundaries, or judgments. There is always room for one more dancer; one more instrument; one more singer. Music embodies the very creativity of God and is heard and felt throughout the entire Universe.

One breath or one heartbeat stands between life and death—or better worded: "More Life." Have confidence in each breath today knowing that it carries within it true life. Remember, the breath of God is infinite! What is your song? What music do you have within that has the potential of inspiring another human being? Don't die without singing your song . . . it is unique, beautiful and filled with the potential to inspire the world around you.

I recently watched a YouTube video of the hallelujah choir singing in the mall. They were all disguised as shoppers in the food court and then the singers broke into the most amazing performance that left onlookers gaping at the talent. So sing your song in life and watch how people respond to that kind of choice; the freedom to live out the music that God has woven within you without any concern to "What will people think."

#20: Take Back Your Ability to Heal
Three things create "dis-ease" within your body: trauma; negative beliefs and toxins.

Did you know you have cancer cells floating around in your body? We all do. A healthy immune system takes care of that for us. How do you create a healthy immune system? Laugh, eat all natural non-toxic foods, avoid sugar, exercise, laugh, release what needs to be released, laugh, forgive what needs to be forgiven, laugh, accept what needs to be accepted, love God, yourself and those around you, lighten up and laugh. Laughter has profound physiological benefits, one of them being a strong immune system. Oh, by the way, the physiological benefits of laughter are available to you, even if it's fake. HAHAHAHA. Laugh every day even if you don't find anything funny.

Heal those false beliefs you have about yourself; remember they are stored at the cellular level (epigenetics). When you heal yourself of your negative patterns of thinking about you and the world around you, the stress will disappear and your immune system will regain its strength to protect you.

Invite God's grace into your healing. Every morning I pray a prayer of confidence: "Thank you God for another day of life to learn how to love better and thank you for my healing." Believe that you will receive that which you ask for. No matter how dark the night gets, choose to surrender all to God. Creativity flows from an acute presence once all worry, doubt and fear cease to exist. Create a beautiful moment today . . . creativity and contentment walk hand in hand. Just as the rain nurtures all of creation, so it is with the challenges of life and our soul. Growth happens in the dark night of the soul.

#21: Laughter Can Save Your Life

Humor and love dissolve rigidity and fear instantly in life.

When you die, you become rigid. When you are alive you move, and live, and have your being in the flow of God's love here on Earth. Laughter flows from within the soul and along with it unleashes healing powers. Studies have shown that laughter boosts immune function by raising levels of infection-fighting T-cells, disease-fighting proteins called Gamma-interferon and B-cells, which produce disease-destroying antibodies; lower blood pressure; reduce stress hormones; and increase muscle flexion. Laughter also triggers the release of endorphins, the body's natural painkillers, producing a general sense of well-being.

Knowing all of this, make it a priority in your day to remain flexible and infuse your sense of humor into all that you do. Don't take yourself or others too seriously. Look for appropriate moments to lighten things up and laugh out loud. Practice laughing. The more you practice the better you will get at it.

Becoming the observer versus the reactor to your life gives you many opportunities to laugh. The antics you and others play in life are quite humorous. Laugh as much as you can throughout your day!

#22: Respect through Suffering
My relationship with my daughter is built on gratitude, love and respect. Because we have walked through this storm together and continued to choose love and life NO MATTER WHAT, we have a very special bond of respect for each other. When I get upset about something *little* in life, she will often say, *"Mom, we know better than that, remember what we have walked through together, don't forget what you learned."* She is wise beyond her years and always has been. The respect came through the experience of life, and life involves suffering, tears, laughter, love and growth. We have experienced it all together. Love walks hand-in-hand with respect. We share both with every breath we take on Earth, knowing that it is a gift.

Respect emerges quickly for a human being when you see suffering of any kind. Suffering evokes vulnerability in the hearts of humanity, along with instant connection. Several of my family members were caught in the 9/11 chaos. One member was running as the building was crumbling and all kinds of debris pelted his back, then everything went black.

A pregnant woman was huddled right outside a revolving door, yet because of the black of dust, she could not see it and collapsed right in front of the open door. My relative grabbed her as he felt his way to the door and pulled her inside to find a janitor cleaning out the eyes of those who had crawled their way inside unable to see. It was a moment of vulnerability through suffering that instantly linked the hearts of humanity.

Suffering does not give preference to class, position, credentials, income, age or race. Yet, it is the portal that when passed through with grace has the potential to connect the hearts of humanity instantly, guiding each participant to a place of vulnerability, which gives birth to love.

Don't fear suffering in life. Shift your perception and look for the gems of love, connection and wisdom that come with it. Don't miss the opportunity for learning and growth in the eye of your storm.

#23: Loss Leads to Perspective

A great loss leaves a great gift behind: Instant perspective on all that is truly important in this life. Craig Morgan has written a country song that speaks to this experience, "This Ain't Nothin'." The lyrics contain a conversation between a reporter and a man who just lost his home in a tornado. The man says losing his home is nothing compared to the loss of the ones he loved during his lifetime.

As with all challenges, many of which are out of your control, you ALWAYS have the choice to grow in the ways of **wisdom** in the midst of it all. The result is "the peace that passes all human understanding." This kind of peace can only be obtained through the experiences of passing through great loss or tribulation. It gives you the opportunity to let go, accept what is and appreciate all that is essential, authentic and good in life. This is a process of life changing healing.

After you obtain a perspective of the essential things in life, you may find that onlookers of your uncommon peace will ask with curiosity, "How can you remain so calm about this, that or the other thing?" These questions will often flow from individuals who have not experienced the gift of perspective in life or those who choose to continue connecting their sense of safety and well-being to the nonessentials.

The ability to see all of life in light of a loss (or tribulation) instantly reduces daily anxiety that often accompanies a lack of perspective. I refer to this as "death bed wisdom." If you have had the opportunity to experience the "kiss of death" in life you know what I am talking about here. This kind of wisdom resonates with profound gratitude for all of life . . . every breath, every heartbeat. Remember, you cannot be grateful and anxious at the same time.

Next time you feel the weight of anxiety, remember all the opportunities in your life that have given you the *gift of perspective* . . . whatever you focus on GROWS BIGGER. I will often pray, "God grant me the grace to remember all that I learned through the storm."

#24: Possibilities from Pain
In the spring of 2010 my husband's mom and dad died suddenly, three weeks apart. As I was contemplating this experience of grief, I was given the following story that has filled my heart with

perspective and peace. Yes, you can grieve and at the same time experience inner peace:

"A talented painter once gave an unforgettable performance in front of an admiring audience. With rapid strokes of his brush, he quickly and skillfully painted a beautiful country scene, replete with green meadows, golden fields of grain, farm buildings in the distance, peaceful trees and a friendly blue sky punctuated with soft, white clouds. As he stepped back from his easel, the audience burst into appreciative applause—only to be silenced by the artist, who announced, "The picture is not complete."

He turned and began rapidly covering the canvas with dark, somber paints. The peaceful country scene was replaced with blotches of morose, unappealing colors, all seemingly thrown on the canvas in random disorder; only a patch of the blue sky and the peaceful countryside remained.

"Now," he asserted, "the picture is finished, and it is perfect." The stunned audience looked on in disbelief; no one understood what had just happened. Then the painter turned the canvas on its side, and the onlookers let out a collective gasp of amazement, for now there appeared before their eyes a stunningly beautiful, dark waterfall, cascading over moss covered rocks and creating a rich symphony of color. The artist intended his amazing and unexpected demonstration to be a commentary, or reflection, on the reality of sorrow: one beautiful scene of life was transformed into another, even as observers believed something wonderful was forever lost. The meaning of this story is simple: God is the artist who created our lives, and who desires to make them into something permanent and glorious; and sorrow and loss are often His instruments in bringing about this change. From our limited perspective, we believe that the original picture is fine as it is and that any change, especially a painful one can only be for the worse.

God however, sees and understands the possibilities of life and eternity far more completely than we ever will and, if we allow it, He can use all the events and experiences of our lives—even the dark and somber ones—to bring about something of lasting and unequaled beauty."[1]

#25: Remove Your Mask of Pain

Victimization often accompanies pain in life. Watch out! You will remain in a place of emotional paralysis as long as you stay in the energy of "why me" or "this is just how it is . . . there is no hope, or this is the way it's always been, so this is the way it will always be."

It's worth exploring the upside to your pain if you desire to release it in life. Who does the disease or pain make you? If you were to guess, what emotional issue lies behind your pain? Have you ever experienced a physical pain clearing up (insomnia, headaches, back pain, etc.) after you have cleared up an emotional issue? Be aware of how powerfully your body manifests your emotional

---

1   Esper, Fr, Joseph M, *More Saintly Solutions to Life's Common Problems.* Sophia Institute Press, May 24, 2004.

pain. It is matchless in its ability to mask or store life's pain or trauma.

Look at the ways you identify with your situation, disease or physical pain in life. What is the upside for you holding onto this in life? How does it serve you? Do you get attention? Do you connect with people who share the same suffering? Special privileges? Excuses from participating in life? What is the benefit for you when it comes to staying in your pain? You will often stay stuck in your undesirable situation when the reason you are stuck is because you desire certain aspects of it. However, it's necessary to identify these excuses in order to make the shift out of your pain. Explore what emotional issues exist behind your situation. Release all victimization and take full ownership of your life.

May your eagerness for growth move you past the obstacles that stand before you, just as the growing flower moves past the elements to reach the warmth of the sun.

#26: Life's Chutes and Ladders®

I went to a seminar once and heard a pain relief specialist, Rick Wilkes, speak about the chutes and ladders of life. He compared moving up the emotional scale to this famous childhood game.

As you make choices to nurture what you value most in life, you become aware of the ladders in life that take you to the next level of emotional stability and inner growth. Events, situations and circumstances, however, will often appear and you find yourself moving rapidly down a "chute" in life, and sitting exactly where you started from, at least from your perception.

Remember that any *chute* that takes you by surprise in life holds within itself the potential for growth. Yes it may shoot you down for a bit, yet you return with wisdom if you choose to be open to it; wisdom that you can now use to avoid similar *chutes* in life and climb up different ladders.

Explore your *board game*. Know that remaining flexible and aware of as many options as possible will empower you to come up with creative solutions to any move you are contemplating making in this life. Wake up and learn from your *chute experiences*. Don't dwell in the past or fixate on your future. Avoid wasting any energy lingering by a closed door that can be spent on seeking the next open window. Ask yourself: "What action can I take right now to find the next ladder of opportunity in my life?"

#27: Visit a Graveyard

"Teach us to number our days aright that we may gain a heart full of wisdom" (Psalm 90:12).

"He who gets wisdom loves his own soul; he who cherishes understanding prospers" (Proverbs 19:8).

Never experienced the brush of death that results in the kiss of life? Visit a hospice, nursing home or graveyard with the intention of gaining wisdom that comes from knowing that you are simply passing through this life for the purpose of learning how to love better. This kind of wisdom leads to profound peace and perspective in all aspects of living.

You want contentment in life? Pursue godliness. You came into this world with no material thing and possessing everything you need for true inner peace. You leave with no material thing. Yet, the only thing you need at that moment exists within every choice you made for love as you walked on this planet we call Earth. You always have everything you need for godliness and true life dwelling within every breath, every heartbeat and every choice for love you make in your day to day living.

Cherish the understanding that comes from numbering your days aright. Become a seeker of the kind of wisdom that guides you to the love of your own soul and those around you, for this is true "deathbed wisdom". Don't wait. Start living it out today.

4

I'M OK, YOU'RE OK ... I'M NOT OK, YOU'RE NOT OK

As Anthony de Mello says, "You see things and people not as they are, but as you are. When you are OK, feeling safe and connected, you have the ability to offer those positive feelings to the world around you. When you are not OK, feeling unsafe and disconnected, you are incapable of offering confidence and love to those around you."

#28: Self-Esteem: Belief in Oneself
Did you know that no two heartbeats are the same? It's true. Heartbeats are as unique as fingerprints. In fact, your heartbeat can be viewed as your energy signature. Energy flows uniquely through each human being. We all give off different vibrations. This is why you have a unique EEG and EKG. Either way, your energy is profoundly

unique. Self-esteem emerges from the awareness of one's own uniqueness. If I asked you to come up on stage and sing a little song you would first consult the writing on your wall. It may say: "Go for it. You were told you were an awesome singer when you sang in the High School choir" ... OR it may say ... "FAT CHANCE, no way I'm getting up there and making a fool out of myself like I did when I sang at church and my mom said I couldn't sing." We are constantly consulting the writing on our walls as we interact with our world. We will be a lot more understanding and open-minded in relationships when we realize that most of our communications with one another come from the writing on our walls.

When the writing on your wall says, "I'm not good enough," everything in your life will be interpreted from this point of view. You will attract events and people who back this "I'm not good enough" belief up until you erase it. So, how do you erase it? Good question. Imagine a table and across the top is written a belief statement about you: I can't sing. The legs of the table represent specific events in your life that back that belief up: My mom said that I can't sing. In order to collapse that belief you must cut down the legs; then the table will fall.

EFT (Emotional Freedom Technique) is an acupressure-based approach to healing. It was pioneered by George Goodheart, DC; John Diamond, MD; and psychologist, Roger Callahan, PhD. Subsequently, it was developed and simplified by Stanford engineer Gary Craig. Effectively, and most times instantly, it assists the healing process.

By emotionally tuning into the specific event, while tapping on precise acupuncture points, the body collapses the "block" that was put in place when you accepted the statement, "I can't sing," as truth.

Many times you only have to tune into one or two *legs* that support your tabletop belief and the whole table crashes down. After using EFT, clients often experience a profound sense of self-worth and peace. As you collapse the different tabletops in your life, a deep awareness of your uniqueness begins to emerge. Belief in yourself begins to replace past negativity . . . once you start *tapping* into this, there is no going back. For more information on this technique, please review the bonus chapter at the end of this book: Getting Your Energy Behind the Shift.

#29: Know Your Body's 'YES' and 'NO'

When to say NO? . . . That's a very good question that I feel we all have asked at one point or another. The key to this is to understand the internal body "Yes" and the internal body "No." As you become familiar with your internal *knowing*, saying no becomes a part of honoring the essence of who you are apart from the opinions of other people.

Once you realize this simple truth: "I am NOT the opinions of other people," it is easy to ask yourself "does this fit with my inner truth and intentions for this day of life?" There is a way to speak the truth in love. Your problem comes when you lose connection with the truth that resides in your heart (due to farming out your identity and self-worth to people, things and circumstances in life).

When you give your power away to another human being and allow them to define you . . . you become a slave to that person . . . you will compromise your inner truth to please them and get positive affirmations and approval from them. You relinquish your ability to say no. This is when you become over committed, overwhelmed and stressed out!

I do specific exercises with my clients to get them in tune with their internal body "Yes" and their internal body "No." It then comes down to giving yourself the gap of empowerment where you step back before committing and ask yourself: "Is this what I WANT to do and have the time to do with love?" rather than "I need to do this in order to be loved and accepted." Once again, it is worth reflecting on what your life would look like if you knew you were loved and accepted no matter what!

#30: Belief in YOU Solves Workplace Anxiety

The American Psychological Association says stress costs corporations $300 billion a year in absences, medical costs, lost productivity, and turnover. 78 percent of American workers feel burned out and a third of Americans say they're living with extreme stress. Nearly 80 percent of all doctor visits are stress-related and 43 percent of adults are sick because of stress.[2]

---

2   American Psychological Association Practice Organization, *Psychologically Healthy*

I'm Ok, You're Ok . . . I'm Not Ok, You're Not Ok

A landmark 20-year study conducted by the University of London concluded that unmanaged reactions to stress were a more dangerous risk factor for cancer and heart disease than either cigarette smoking or high cholesterol foods.[3] Get the picture? Workplace stress not only costs money; it costs lives. Stress is a silent killer and one of the top stressors that occur in the workplace: "Oh no, what if I lose my job? I stress out every time I have to speak, travel, complete a project by a deadline, or have a performance review."

What if you know that no matter what situation you find yourself in at work two beliefs will direct your responses? "I am OK just as I am, and I am capable of handling any situation before me." How would that shift your perception? And the other little cure for stress reduction is this: become a curious and fascinated human being versus a human being who needs to analyze, interpret and conclude at every turn in life.

I'm sure you have heard this statement: "When one door closes another opens." Become a seeker of open doors at work and in life. Remain flexible and be willing to remember YOU in the midst of

Workplace Program Fact Sheet: By the Numbers, 2010. Retrieved from http://www.apa.org/practice/programs/workplace/phwp-fact-sheet.pdf

3   Cryer, B. (1996). *Neutralizing Workplace Stress: The Physiology of Human Performance and Organizational Effectiveness*. Presented at: Psychological Disabilities in the Workplace, The Centre for Professional Learning, Toronto, CA. June 12, 1996.

it all: your talents, gifts, insights, humor, abilities, uniqueness and creativity. Fear of *what people will think* is enough to cause you to forget all the value you bring to your company simply because you are you. What if you woke up tomorrow and went to work without any fear as to the response of your co-workers? Simply grounding yourself in what you know to be true and valuable is enough to release on the job stress.

Make confidence and love your foundation in all you do. Take nothing personally today, knowing that anything anyone says or does flows from their own journey.

#31: Stay in Your Castle

St. Teresa of Avila wrote a masterpiece called: "The Interior Castle" where she refers to the soul as the interior castle with many rooms. God dwells at the center of the soul. If you desire to see, hear and respond to life from a place of inner peace, wisdom and love it is essential to *remain in your castle* where you experience safety and connection, which grounds the experience of love in all that you experience on Earth. St. Teresa concluded:

"It is love alone that gives worth to all things. To have courage for whatever comes in life—everything lies in that."

Remember that two of your essential needs for inner peace flow from the experience of safety and connection. When you explore the many rooms of your soul (the different aspects of you), committed to deleting all false beliefs and bondage to past pain (why did this happen, I can't forgive, I can't let go), your safety and courageous confidence will return.

When you are in *your castle* you remember what is true; honorable, praise worthy and of value. When you move against anything that is important to you in life, anxiety will appear.

Remain in your castle as you go through your day, connected to God and what you know to be true about yourself. You may say, "I don't know what is true about me." In this case, ask yourself what you find to be beautiful in life. What captures your heart when you see it, hear it, feel it or experience it? Again, what moves you to tears? All of your answers to these questions will help you to remember the truth about yourself as connected to God.

#32: Collaboration Over Competition

The difference between competition and collaboration in life is the difference between working together for a greater good and working for one's own advantage in life. I choose collaboration because it feels a lot better and the results inspire confidence and inner creativity verses fear and frustration, which often accompanies competition in the workplace and in life.

Have you ever noticed how the songs that flow from the birds of nature seem to be void of all competition, the kind that results in envy and jealousy? It seems to be enough to simply join in the beautiful symphony of life having full confidence in the unique harmony they bring into this world. May it be the same for us.

The same holds true for spring flowers. The smallest viola that radiates its brilliant purple color does not seem threatened by the grand stature of the sunflower. Nor does the daffodil shrink back in the presence of the lily whose fragrance swallows up any small hint of scent that the daffodil puts forth. The wisdom contained in nature has no need for envy or jealousy in the midst of the beauty that springs forth in God's master landscape of life and love.

Accepting yourself, all that you are, just as you are opens the doors of connection, appreciation and love. Rather than living by the internal lists you carry, "I will accept myself when . . ." "I will love myself when . . ." "I will be successful when . . ." explore the experience of accepting yourself now. In that choice to accept you, you will find that love will bloom in all aspects of your life. You will experience life as the "lilies of the field" do . . . the freedom to simply be.

In the freedom to be, experience, creativity, inspiration and motivation bloom within the soul. Gratitude and appreciation for all of life begin to take root over the emotional paralysis that flows from envy, jealousy and coveting. This is a huge source of stress in your life, and it serves no one; especially not you.

Today, begin to embrace the experience of your own unique note that you play in this symphony of life. You will begin to notice how all the notes together create the song of God in this world.

God grant us grace to have the eyes to see, the ears to hear and the heart to respond to the beauty of life that resides within and around us each day of life.

#33: Release Leads to Peace
As you enter another day of life, what if you could release all that blocks you from experiencing love in your life?

Each new day of life offers you the opportunity to begin again, if you choose to embrace this opportunity. Making the choice for that which leads to peace within your soul always involves the experience of surrender and release.

Below are opportunities for growth that may ultimately lead to a profound sense of inner peace and love.

Explore what speaks to you today:

- Surrendering all to God, releasing your need to understand why.
- Letting go of feeling taken advantage of or used.
- Embrace gratitude as a lifestyle.
- I feel most loved when? (Make a list of all that evokes a sense of love within.)
- I feel most accepted when? (Make a list of all that evokes a sense of acceptance within.)
- Let go of resentment and anger. (Anger is linked to fear, fear that you won't be safe, capable or able to handle life situations.)

- Let go of your need for certain outcomes in order to feel good.
- Let go of playing the victim in life. Make the choice to use that energy to come up with creative solutions to life situations.

The more I release my need to know . . . the more I seem to know; and peace comes with it.

#34: Remember Your Worth!

Feelings of inadequacy can cause emotional paralysis in all areas of life. Feeling fear around the thought of really going for it in life is directly linked to feelings of unworthiness or inadequacy.

Ever have this internal conversation: "I'm capable . . . No, I'm not . . . Yes, I am . . . No, I'm not." Close your eyes and imagine your life on a time line. Observe this timeline as if you are floating above it. Ask yourself: When was the first time in my life when I felt inadequate, incapable or overlooked? Imagine that holograph from your past with as much detail as possible.

Now, allow yourself to drift to a time in your life that happened before your "inadequacy realization moment." Pick a time on your timeline when you felt completely validated, capable and more than adequate. Imagine that you have the ability to take all of those positive feelings and pull them through your entire timeline, moving through each event that triggered your feelings of inadequacy; replacing all feelings of inadequacy with confidence and capable feelings. Bring that positive vibration all the way up to today. Now imagine your life going forward having remembered your worth. What would you notice different in your day-to-day events moving from a place of inner confidence and capability? How would your interactions with people around you shift? What would you dare to do in your life with this resurrected remembrance of your capabilities and worth?

#35: Shift Your Focus: Shift Your Life

The co-founders of Neuro Linguistic Programming (NLP) are Richard Bandler and linguist John Grinder. NLP is a powerful stress relief practice. It helps you connect to more available options and perceptions, which instantly reduce stress. Below are a few NLP insights:

- **Neuro:** All behavior flows from your neurological processes of hearing, taste, smell, sight, touch . . . basically you experience the world through your five senses, you make sense of it and then act on it.

- **Linguistic:** You use language to organize your thoughts and behavior and then to communicate. Pacing and leading leads to rapport and instant connection. Body language: 55%; Voice Tonality 38%; Words 7 %. *Watch out for the writing on your wall, huge block to connection.*

- **Programming:** The ways or methods you choose to organize your actions and ideas to create results in life. When you reprogram, your perception of life shifts.

- **Outcome:** Know what you want; create a clear focus of your outcome in the situation. Use visualization gets all five senses involved (lemon exercise: imagine eating a lemon. What is your physiological response from this visualization? Know the power of your thoughts on your body).

- **Acuity:** Keep all of your senses open so that you are acutely aware of what you're getting. The way to do what you want to do already exists, you simply need to tune into it! Become a curious human being vs. a reactive human being.

- **Flexibility:** Here is a popular NLP adage: "If you always do what you've always done, you'll always get what you've always got. If what you're doing is not working . . . do something else."

#36: Personal Peace Process

As mentioned earlier, EFT (Emotional Freedom Technique) is a very powerful stress relief technique that can be applied to anything in life that causes you emotional or physical discomfort. The EFT instructions are found in the bonus chapter at the end of this book.

Below is a process created by Gary Craig, the founder of EFT, and is a very powerful stress relief tool.

Personal Peace Procedure:

Make a list of every bothersome-specific event you can remember.

1. While making your list you may find that some events don't seem to cause you any

current discomfort. That's OK. List them anyway. The mere fact that you remember them suggests a need for resolution.

2. Give each specific event a title, as though it was a mini-movie. Examples:

   a. Dad hit me in the kitchen.

   b. My brother threw a snake on me when I was 10.

   c. I almost slipped and fell into the Grand Canyon.

   d. Mom locked me in a closet for two days.

   e. Bill held me under water when I was five.

   f. Mrs. Adams told me I was stupid.

3. When the list is complete, pick out the biggest redwoods in your negative forest and apply EFT to each of them until you either laugh about it or can't think about it anymore. Be sure to notice any aspects that may come up and consider them separate trees in your negative forest. Apply EFT to them accordingly. Be sure to keep after each event until it is resolved.

If you cannot get a 0-10 intensity level on a particular movie then assume you are repressing it and apply 10 full rounds of EFT on it from every angle you can think of. This gives you a high possibility for resolving it. After the big redwoods have been removed, go to the next biggest trees.

4. Do at least one movie (specific event) per day preferably three . . . for three months. It only takes minutes per day. At this rate, you will have resolved 90 to 270 specific events in three months.

Now, notice how much better your body feels. Note too, that your threshold for getting upset is much lower. Note how your relationships are better and how many of your therapy type issues just don't seem to be there anymore. Revisit some of those specific events and notice how those previously intense incidences have vanished. Note any improvements in your blood pressure, pulse and breathing ability.

I ask you to consciously notice these things because, unless you do, the quality healing you will have undergone will seem so subtle that you may not notice it. You may even dismiss it saying, "Oh well. It was never much of a problem anyway." This happens repeatedly with EFT, and thus I bring it to your awareness.

DID YOU KNOW YOU'RE AN ADDICT?

#37: The Drug of Approval

Once again, I draw on the profound wisdom that comes from my spiritual mentor Anthony de Mello.

Whenever you cling to anything in this life—whether it is a certain response from the world; a relationship; a material item or desired outcome—happiness dies and anxiety increases.

Since you were little you began to learn very quickly what to do and say to get a desired outcome or response, and your addiction to the drug of approval began. It is similar to a spoiled child, the more you give it, the more it wants. This addiction to approval is fed by your desire to be acknowledged, approved of, popular, validated and praised. It is as if you are saying, "Please tell me that I am good enough, appreciated, smart enough and worthy to be loved and accepted."

It is a serpent of a drug and will sap you of any remembrance that you already have everything you truly need within your soul for happiness to occur; along with inner peace and joy. It makes a mockery out of you with the antics you play in life all for a momentary high of being approved of or acknowledged.

Being a visionary and motivated human being is of considerable value. It is when you look to those around you to tell you that you can or cannot do something in life, or you only believe in yourself because someone told you how great you are, that you become vulnerable to the experience of forgetting who you are with your God given inner strengths and abilities.

It is a wonderful practice in life to maintain inner calm and connection in the presence of praise or criticism. In this experience, you are able to remain in *your castle* (connected to God). Remember as with any addiction in life, the more you feed it, the more it consumes you along with your ability to remember who you truly are.

#38: Stuck in Your Attachments?
Want happiness to return? Release all attachment . . . the need for certain outcomes in order to feel good about you. When you desire anything in life in order to feel good about you, it becomes a threat which ultimately leads to the fear of not getting it or losing it.

Did You Know You're An Addict?

In one of Anthony de Mello's lectures, he said,

> *If your happiness depends on anyone or anything, that's anxiety, tension not happiness that's pressure; that's fear. Love is not a desire. A desire leads to a threat and then fear. Whenever you have a strong emotion, positive or negative, it's not possible to see the other person clearly.*

Of course, that's because your strong emotions block you from seeing the unseen. Strong emotions often accompany attachments because the attachment is fueled by the thought: "I won't be okay if I don't get this." One of the three legs of fear is that you feel you are not safe.

Clear off your lens that has been fogged by your false beliefs, then your attachments in life will drop and peace will return.

> *Clarity of perception equals accuracy of response. You will never live until you stop clinging to life.* **—Anthony de Mello**

#39: Who Wrote on Your Wall?

Remember the writing on your wall? When you give your pen away to another human being to write a message (that you believe is true) on your interior *wall,* and you leave it there and consult that writing as you go through your life, you disconnect from your inner truth. The problem comes when that writing is negative and you see the world through that negative lens.

Below are a few questions to ask yourself to help you explore what kind of writing you are consulting everyday:

> Who would I be without my wounds?
>
> Who have I given permission to in my life to define who I am?
>
> What circumstances in my life have I given permission to define me? Circumstances that represent a block in my ability to accept all that I am, just as I am.
>
> Who did I give my pen over to in my life . . . giving them permission to write on my internal wall of beliefs about me?
>
> What do I need around me in my life to feel safe being me . . . me, just as I am?

#40: The Prison of: What Will Other People Think?

Are you imprisoned by the "what will other people think" dilemma? You're not alone. Most human beings develop this fear, creating their own prison, which prevents the expression of their true self. Can you imagine if you woke up tomorrow and this worry was not even on your radar? How would that shift your expressions and reactions to the world around you? It's worth exploring that question.

Any time you get yourself in the vibration of a new thought pattern using your imagination you access the subconscious beliefs or that writing on your interior wall. As you imagine, "Wow, what *would* my life look like if I could let that fear, worry or doubt go?" Write down what you think you would notice that would be different in terms of how you interact with other people if you no longer entertained the thought "What will other people think?" before responding to the world around you. What new found freedoms would you reconnect with about yourself?

It's worth becoming aware of when this worry plays out in your life. As you begin your day, choose to become the observer of this crazy block that prevents you from being you in this world. Then imagine, "What if I responded without the fear of what others would think?" I would imagine you would experience a lot more light hearted moments and laughter . . . at yourself and situations. Try it; it's a liberating experience that leads to inner peace and calm.

#41: Are You a "Take Everything Personally" Addict?

Taking things personally, that other people do or say, evokes a ton of stress and anxiety among humanity in day-to-day living!

Working with people who are angry, difficult and "acting out their pain" in life is probably one of the most amazing opportunities for you to practice the art of "taking nothing any human being says or does personally." Think about it, what would your life look like if you could remain connected to a place of safety within while being surrounded by a bunch of *sharks* in the workplace? How would that shift your experience of peace in the midst of chaos?

Believe me, it takes practice and a lot of inner dialogue to stand before a human who is throwing up all of their life frustrations in front of you. When you take the position of the *observer* versus the *reactor* you give yourself the opportunity and space to choose your response. When you realize, truly realize, and embrace the truth that any negative thing a human being does, has everything to do with their past pain or fears of the future and you just happen to be in the way, you are free to identify and adjust your perception of the situation.

I encourage my clients to play the inner narrator, when surrounded by angry, frustrated people which actually becomes quite humorous: "Wow, look at this human being unloading all of their trash in front of me . . . look at how red their face is getting, that looks uncomfortable . . . I wonder how they got to be so angry in life? . . . Oh well, it has nothing to do with me, I'm not going to give them the power to rock my boat today." When you have a spirit of curiosity and fascination versus attachments and assumptions, you will find an endless reservoir of opportunity for learning and growth while staying grounded.

The bottom line; don't give your power away to any human being. You only feel inferior by your own consent; you can apply this to any emotional response.

#42: It's Not Rejection, It's Just Direction
I use this mantra every day. It helps to diffuse not taking everything personally. I started using this mantra when I was looking for an agent and

got a ton of "great work, but no thanks" response letters. When I chose to take the perspective of: "My work must not fit in with their agenda for this year," I was able to keep on going for it without that dreaded feeling of: "something must be wrong with me or my work."

I remember as I opened the "no thank you" letters . . . before my mind even had a minute to connect to the inner critic, I would start the mantra: "It's not rejection it's just direction." I would follow it up with: "If not here then where? Where is the open door? I know it's out there I just have to tune into it." Be a seeker and keep on knocking, perhaps on a different door, and you will find what you are looking for.

I remember memorizing a verse in college that has given me a lot of confidence when it comes to those "closed door" experiences in life. It speaks of the guidance that is available to all of us, all the time. We simply need to remove the static of our fearful emotions, doubts and worries enough to hear it: "Whether you turn to the right or to the left, your ears will hear a voice behind you, saying, 'This is the way; walk in it'" (Isaiah 30:21).

#43: The "I'll Get to It Tomorrow" Rut

Stop procrastinating; stop procrastinating . . . why are you procrastinating? Waiting until the last minute to get 100 things done causes stress. If you can do it now then do it: make that call, write that letter, take action on the life in front of your face.

Remember that you are not the responses from the world around you. Many procrastinators are also perfectionists. Much of the delay in getting it done has to do with the fear that the end product will not be good enough. Remember the famous quote from an unknown author: *"What would you dare to do if you knew you could not fail?"*

Watch out for the inner critic in the midst of your procrastination. Rather than being critical of yourself become curious as to the reason behind putting something off. Is it fear of failure? Too much on your plate? Perhaps this is an invitation to prioritize in your life and release some nonessentials in order to create more time for what you value most.

Now, some of your work on earth is just part of the deals you make in life. Ask yourself when you are in a paralysis rut due to procrastination: "What action can I take right now on this project?" Focus on small actions that you can take right now toward your goal. As Confucius says *"A journey of a thousand miles begins with one step."*

#44: Simplify and Organize Your Life
How do you feel inside after you have done a *spring cleaning?* . . . this, by the way, can be done any time of the year? It often brings about clarity of thinking and a sense of inner calm. You can spring clean something every day. Ask yourself: "What is essential for me to live in this particular space? How can I de-clutter in order to bring more clarity and efficiency as I live and move throughout my day?"

Basically, when you remove those things, in any space, that distract you from what is essential to accomplishing your tasks, or simply being; you will find that clarity of thinking, calm and focus will return. Impaired cognitive thinking is one of the many side effects of stress along with decreased productivity. When you create an environment for yourself that is clutter free then you actually release the inner stress that often accompanies the, "I can't find anything in this mess" syndrome.

Choose a time to de-clutter when you are not in a panic to find a certain piece of information or item. Take advantage of a calm moment when there is nothing pressing you. Breathe deeply and take one small spot at a time.

I must add that I have learned the benefits of creating a de-cluttered life after being a clutter-junky for many years. It makes life so much easier, less complicated and peaceful when you know where everything is, and you remove all the items that are non-essentials in life . . . like the yo-yo that has no string on it that you have continually pushed out of the way in a desperate attempt to find what you are looking for in your desk. Let it go!

#45: The Lying Addiction: It's More Common than You Think

This is an easy entry for me to write about because I used to do it all the time; particularly, as a teenager.

Did you know that you lie (I'm talking about any kind of bending of the truth) because you are afraid of what other people will think or how they may react if you told them the truth? Or, you are afraid you won't get ahead in life; be acknowledged or approved of. This fear flows from your deeper fear that you will not be able to handle their response to you or the outcome as a result of speaking your truth.

You fear strong negative emotional responses from people. They are only negative because of the writing on your wall. If one of your messages happens to be: "It is never okay to express your anger," then you will avoid that situation as much as possible, even if you have to lie your way out of a confrontation.

What if you knew that you were capable of handling any response from any human being no matter what you told them? How would that affect the times when you "bend the truth" in order to avoid confrontation?

I have yet to meet a human being who has said, "I love confrontation, especially when it involves strong emotions, yelling and maybe even crying."

I have also never met a human being who has worked through a challenging confrontation, remained grounded in their truth, compassionate in their responses and open to a solution, that has not emerged feeling relieved and at peace.

When you are not aligned with your truth, stress multiplies in your body. Practice speaking the truth in love. It is an art in this life that requires a courageous, persistence choice for truth over falsehood yet the result is a life of integrity worth every effort. Be a seeker of truth. Remember the words of Dr. David Hawkins: *"Peace is the natural state when truth prevails."*

THE BOAT OR JESUS

We all have our "boat" of safety in life where many of us remain simply because it's familiar. What is your boat of safety and have you ever stepped out of it to explore unknown waters?

#46: Practice Living Life
You have a lot of anxiety over new situations in life. To regain balance in your life, simply shift your perception from: "In order to be loved and accepted I need to do this perfectly," to "I am willing to love and accept myself even though I don't do everything perfectly; I am willing to practice living life without fear." As with failure, the word "perfect" is subjective to each human being.

Make a list of everything you are consciously aware of that needs to happen in *your perceived stressful situation* in order for you to feel good about yourself. For example, you have an interview coming up and a lot of anxiety around the thought: "What if I don't say what they want to hear in order for me to get this job offer." That fearful thought has a list of perfection attached to it. How about this thought: "Okay, I have this interview. I'm nervous, but I'm willing to accept myself anyway. I am willing to explore feeling good about myself. I am confident and capable, with or without this interview." This shift in focus when used with some EFT (see Getting Your Energy Behind the Shift bonus chapter at the end of the book) is enough to realign you with your truth: you are entirely capable of handling any and every situation that unfolds before you in life. When you look at all of life as an opportunity to practice living on earth and remember your God given strength and abilities, it takes the pressure of needing to be perfect off your plate.

Contemplate the little child living out the freedom of simply being alive. When you look at new experiences as practice, you open yourself up to opportunities for growth. Practice your ability to connect; communicate, reach out, listen, share, give, receive, and focusing on what you want. The skills you practice will grow in the areas of spontaneity, flexibility and creativity. Exploring different ways to do things in life reconnects you to your inner inspirations, and the wonderment of life returns.

I was observing a kindergarten class walking in from recess. Each little person chose a different way to travel into that school. I saw everything from skipping to hopping on one foot, both feet, walking backwards, holding hands, spinning in circles or every few steps stopping and balancing on one foot. Reconnect to your inner child who has not forgotten the excitement that comes from exploring and practicing new ways to see and live life.

#47: Failure is a Perspective

Did you know that failure is simply a label you use when you don't get certain desirable outcomes in life? When something happens in life that you feel is insufficient or falls short of your expectations or assumptions of how it was supposed to be, from your perception, you often label it as a failure; this can lead to "less than" feelings about yourself or others.

If you can watch for this in life and choose to observe yourself making these kinds of choices (to label undesirable outcomes as failure), you give yourself the opportunity to reframe into a positive. Whenever you choose to reframe any negative response or label in life into a positive, you open yourself up to creative solutions.

Often you say to yourself, "I can't do that!" This automatic response instantly aligns yourself with your experience of failure. How about saying, "I just don't know how to do that yet, but I have confidence in my ability to learn." Words are powerful in terms of their ability to link you to your false beliefs and past pain. In turn, they are just as powerful to help you link to your God given strength and abilities to overcome.

Part of moving through those moments in life that you label as "failure" is to practice the prayer of serenity. *"God grant me the grace to accept the things I cannot change, the courage the change the things I can and the wisdom to know the dif-*

ference." Any time you resist what is before you, you set yourself up for remaining *stuck* in life. Yes, you will remain in a place of emotional paralysis each time you do not accept the things you cannot change.

So, you got let go from your job. You can label that as a failure if you like, or you can focus on the "let go" part of the experience. Now you are free to pursue that next open door. Be vigilant over your labels in situations like this in life. Use your delete key to remove all negative self-talk and replace it with the positive.

Know that whatever label you chose to define a situation in life will directly affect the outcome.

#48: You Can Walk on Top of Water

One of my favorite bible stories takes place on water with a boat, the disciples and Jesus. (Matthew 14:22-35)

Jesus, told his disciples to get into a boat and head to the other side of the lake. The wind happened to be against them so you can imagine it wasn't easy. At that time in history, The Romans divided the night into four "watches" of three hours each. Jesus decided to go to the disciples, walking on top of the water, at the forth watch of the night. After fighting the wind all night you can be sure that there was considerable anxiety among the men on the boat. To top it off, they see a man walking towards them, ON the water! Talk about a stressful situation. They all were terrified thinking that Jesus was a ghost. Immediately, Jesus says to them, *"Take courage it is I, don't be afraid."* Passionate Peter jumps up and says, *"Lord, if it's you, tell me to come to you on the water."* So, of course Jesus tells him to come. Now, as with any new challenge in life, a part of you is excited and eager to explore these new opportunities. Yet, all too often as you begin walking through the challenge you become distracted by your fears, doubts and worries. You begin to focus on the wind and waves around you, and as you do you begin to sink. As soon as Peter saw the wind and waves his fear caused him to sink. Jesus responded by grabbing his hand and pulling him out. Jesus only words to Peter were profound: *"You of little faith, why did you doubt?"*

Often God comes to you in the fourth watch of the night when you are fearful, tired and broken inviting you to surrender all and trust in your ability to rise above the storm. As you remember the source of your greatest abilities and strengths in the midst of the waves and wind, all things become possible for you. What would it take for you to step out of your boat and explore your ability to walk on top of water?

#49: Living Outside Your Boat
Your boat or "box" is your place where you hang out because it is familiar to you and whatever is familiar to you gives you a sense of safety. Unfortunately, many times your boat contains items that have the potential of sinking your boat rather than moving you forward in life. Think of your boat or place of safety that you have created for yourself. What items (beliefs, behaviors or habitual responses) in life no longer serve your well-being and inner growth? It's worth making a list of the

things that you could benefit from by throwing them overboard.

Now, once you have done some boat cleaning, you are ready to look out over the horizon and consider venturing out into unfamiliar waters. Know this, each time you choose to open yourself up to expansion in life—once you expand—it is very seldom that you will go back to your old boat. Imagine that you can walk on top of water wherever you want to go. Once you have that experience, why would you go back to sitting in your old boat? You go back because it's familiar. Practice exploring what is unfamiliar to you. As you do, you will begin to feel more confident exploring the unknown.

The next time you come face-to-face with a new situation and you are tempted to stay in your boat, imagine what awaits you as you choose to venture out into uncharted waters. Enter life as a whole human being with your eyes and heart wide open.

When they told me I had a 50 percent chance of survival I gave myself permission to reconnect to all that I let go of or compromised as a result of pain and false beliefs in my life.

Another phrase for living outside of your box (or boat) could be: living outside of the connection you made with the pain and patterns of behavior that no longer serve you or anyone around you in this life. When you link to your pain and give it permission to define you in life you will remain in your boat. It's your choice to live outside your *box*. Practice taking little steps each day to step out of your comfort zone. The more you practice the easier it becomes. All of life will begin to come alive before you!

#50: Stop the Craze of Addictions and Cravings

Addictions and cravings in life have many different faces, yet the same result: they block your ability to remember that you can choose your response to life and your ability to remain connected to your authentic self as connected to God (you before all the pain and false beliefs kicked in).

According to Webster, an addiction is to give oneself over to a strong habit, and a craving is to long for something eagerly. "I need to have this thing, outcome or person in order to feel relief, calm or momentary peace within," is a common thought linked to addictions and cravings.

Honoring the physiological component of a craving is also an important ingredient to overcoming the "eagerly longing for" moments in life. Low serotonin levels have been linked to physical challenges, including migraines, depression, lack of concentration and insomnia. Your body makes serotonin from tryptophan.

Where do you get tryptophan? Sugars/Carbohydrates . . . not a good choice and the results often times are more cravings . . . "I can't just have one Oreo™ cookie; I need to devour the entire sleeve!" . . . Of course you do, sugar is addicting; as are carbs.

Don't stress yourself out when you observe this kind of behavior in your life. Just know your body is trying to balance itself. You play a major part in that process by choosing healthy foods that satisfy your body's need for the essential amino acid, tryptophan, in order to boost your serotonin levels. Help your body help you. Go for the turkey, cottage cheese, black eyed-peas, eggs and almonds. Buy a little wheat germ and put it over some cottage cheese. You will find that your addictions and cravings around food will be replaced by inner balance and peace as your serotonin levels are balanced due to healthy choices.

Also, be aware of the emotional component woven into an addiction or craving in life. Just as the sugar will **momentarily** satisfy your body's craving for the tryptophan, the emotional high that you have given yourself over to, in order to feel good about you, will invariably be followed by an equal **low**.

What have you given yourself over to in life? Do any of these sound familiar? In order to feel good about me or safe in this world I need:

- To have certain material things
- To be heard and understood, right and accepted.
- To have an obsessive order around me
- Words of affirmation, affection and acknowledgment
- Certain foods/drinks
- Perfection from myself, others or both

Beware of the ATTACHMENT craze in life. Anthony de Mello says that an attachment is an emotional state of clinging due to the belief that without some particular person, thing or outcome you cannot be happy. It is cyclical. The thrill of getting that which you are attached to is followed closely behind by the anxiety that comes from the fear that you will lose that which you are attached to.

Try this: Take one day at a time and practice living without attachment to the work of your hands. Do what you do and then let it go and embrace the moment in front of your face.

#51: Resurrect Your Voice
Did you forget how to speak your truth in life? How to say no when you have too much on your plate? How to speak up when you feel taken advantage of or when you have something to say?

If this is the case, you are carrying the stress of silence around in your body. The kind of silence I'm talking about here is when you swallow your truth for the sake of honoring one of your inner beliefs about yourself that does not promote inner balance and well-being. The beliefs usually sound like this: "What I have to say isn't important. I'll sound stupid if I speak up. I risk being rejected or undermined if I speak."

All of these beliefs could be flowing from a childhood tribal agreement: "Children are to be seen and not heard." Or "Only speak when you are spoken to." Or "You have experienced negative feedback as a result of speaking." Again, when you have given away the power to define you and your actions, you have the ability to take it back.

Try this reframe: "Even though it wasn't safe to speak my truth when I was young, I am willing to love and accept myself. I choose to resurrect my voice along with confidence in speaking my truth freely. I am willing to consider this: that was then and this is now, and I have a lot more resources available to me to reconnect to the parts of me that I disconnected from in order to survive in my world as a child."

If you are moved from within to share, then practice speaking up in your life. Your voice is simply the portal through which the inspiration held within your heart speaks. The word "inspiration" is derived from the Latin verb *inspiro* which means "to breathe on" or "to breathe into." According to Webster, inspiration means to "motivate by divine influence." Reconnect to your inner voice of inspiration and explore, allowing it to inspire those around you. Your spirit knows no fear. Your fears flow from your perceptions that label events or situations as threatening.

#52: Are You Addicted to Your Trauma?

Some of you have been hit by huge tsunamis in this life which often come after an eerie period of calm. How you choose to link your self-image to your tsunami makes all the difference in the replay experience for the rest of your life.

If you remember that *who you are* stands separate from any event, circumstance or situation in life, then the calm will return after the storm. However, if you link any part of your sense of self-worth or identity to the sickness, abuse, abandonment, or traumatic event, you will continue to attract people, events and situations into your life that back up that link. Basically, it will continue to show up, different characters, venues and details yet the same theme. In some cases, the trauma has become so ingrained in your identity that you forget who you truly are and that you have the ability to heal.

#53: Clean Out Your Matrix

The Matrix is just another name for what quantum physicists call the Quantum Field or Your Energy Field. It has also been referred to as the Divine Matrix. It is how God wove you together, energetically speaking. We use EEGs and EKGs to track the energy of the brain and heart. You give off energy and your energy can become depleted through exposure to other electrical fields. This is why such devices as Q-Links are so popular. They diffuse outside electrical fields that interfere with yours. Because of the hours I spend in front of the computer, I wear one every day.

The impact of your negative beliefs is actually stored in your matrix. Which is done through imprinting (taking on characteristics of your parents through observation and imitation), most of which are taken on between birth and six years of age. You create thoughts and behaviors which then become habitual patterns stored in local fields. EFT Master Karl Dawson has some powerful insights into this method.

Karl's technique of Matrix Re-imprinting focuses on your inner child and other moments when life-altering decisions were made. Again, the use of EFT with this technique results in powerful emotional and physical transformations.

Some of the most powerful work in terms of releasing the negative beliefs about yourself occurs when you go back to a specific event on your time line when you first recall particular beliefs entering your radar. Once you have picked this short scene out from your life, you imagine yourself dialoging with *you* at that specific moment in time. Basically, you are reconnecting with part of your neurology that splits off in order to isolate a traumatic event that was unbearable to your conscious mind, due to the lack of emotional resources, at that time.

You become triggered repeatedly from these scenes in your past that still hold a negative charge for you. This is because your unconscious mind and heart see them as current events. What memories do you have that are still current events affecting your day to day life? As you reflect on specific childhood events that created your "holographs", identify which decisions made you unique?

Again, step out of the situation and observe. You are capable of creating a new association with your inner child; a new movie.

#54: I Have To Be Perfect . . . OR ELSE!
Really? Or else what? You won't be worthy of love and acceptance? It's worth looking into because when you embrace yourself just as you are with or without needing things to be a certain way in order to feel good about yourself, peace returns.

Talk about setting up a stressful environment in your interior *house*. What if you could let it go? Where did you learn that you need to be perfect in order to feel good about yourself? Whose face is behind this belief? How does it affect your life? Have you allowed this pattern of behavior to define you because you have a fear that if you let it go you would not know who you are? Believe it or not, that is enough to keep you stuck in this exhausting pattern of behavior based on illusory expectations.

What beliefs from your past does this *need to be perfect* flow from? Once you identify it, you have what EFT (see bonus chapter at the end of the book for this technique) refers to as, "a tapable issue."

The next time you feel the compulsion to prove that you are good enough, through perfection, try plugging your scene into this template: "Even though my dad told me I wasn't capable of doing a good enough job after I washed the windows when I was 8, I am willing to love and accept myself today. I realize that my Dad was doing the best he could with the resources he had at the time, and so was I. I choose to believe that my best in life in enough. I am good enough just as I am."

THESE TWO COMMANDMENTS CAN TRANSFORM YOUR LIFE

Jesus was once approached by one of the teachers of the law and asked which commandment was the greatest, to which Jesus replied, "Love the Lord your God with all your heart and with all your soul and with all your mind and with all your strength. The second is this: Love your neighbor as yourself, there is no commandment greater than these." This teaching appears in Mark 12:30 and many other times in the Bible.

#55: You Give What You Want
Gary D. Chapman wrote a wonderful book entitled *The Five Love Languages.* Physical Touch, Acts of Service, Gifts, Quality Time and Words

of Affirmation. In my short experience with love in life, I have found that I speak and desire love verbally and physically. I also give out in my relationships what I want to get. The problem occurs when my partner doesn't feel loved by the language of love I am giving and does not know how to speak the language I desire.

If you give out (and desire) physical touch by someone whose main love language is acts of service, you will create a huge energy shortage when it comes to your heart connection. Until you learn how to speak your partner's main love language instead of giving out what you want to get, you will continue to experience tension and disconnect in your relationship.

Using your fingertips to tap on certain main switches in your body (EFT, see the bonus chapter at the end of the book) frees you to collapse any negative charges you might have around your own experiences with love. By doing this you free up your body's energy system, enabling it to be open to new expressions of love. As soon as you realign yourself with a place of safety and connection to God you will unleash creative ways to give and receive love, taking your partner's love language into consideration.

When you reduce the negativity within your own energy system, you bring out your natural God-given propensity to see the beauty in others. EFT helps to collapse any judgments and conditional criteria you have gained and used throughout your lifetime that supports your interpretation of love.

Key Point: IT'S YOUR INTERPRETATION OF LOVE. Even though your partner does not give and receive love the way you do, you can deeply and completely love and accept yourself anyway. Then, you will enable yourself up to experiencing new expressions of love. In addition you can choose to bring to light creative ways to communicate your love needs.

Love evokes love. Acceptance evokes acceptance. Yes, you give what you want and what you have within to give. When you love yourself well, that love helps to unleash acceptance of others. This in turn collapses judgments you have gathered around love and acceptance. You can then enter a whole new dimension: *emotional freedom* in love for the sake of love alone.

#56: Who Would You Be Without Your Wounds?

Who would you be without your wounds? Because you have spent much of your life nurturing your wounds and attaching a sense of your identity to them, it is often a scary experience to think about your life without them. Who would you be? What would change in your life if you left your wounds behind? How have you used your wounds to justify your anger, fear, worry or doubt? How have you used your wounds to validate your life purpose? Many times you will say: "I deserve this, because I have suffered so much." Living in a state of, "I deserve this" is actually linked to victimization and will keep you stuck in life. However, when you choose, in spite of your wounds, a spirit of gratitude and curiosity, you open yourself to healing and a forward momentum in life. "How can I grow and learn how to love better through my wounds? How can I use my wounds to connect to the hearts of humanity and inspire them in the midst of their wounds?"

Again, when you remember that you are not what is outside of you, including your wounds, you give yourself an open door to reconnect to your true self as connected to God. You can then love yourself and neighbor from a place of empowerment versus victimization, which holds within itself the potential to move mountains.

#57: Success Is Not a Secret
Jesus asked two blind men: *"What do you want me to do for you?"* This question has always intrigued me because obviously Jesus could *see* that they were blind. This speaks to a deeper element here that is essential to healing: belief and faith. Jesus could not perform miracles in His hometown because they did not believe He could. Faith is an essential ingredient to unleash the healing in life.

Do you want to experience success? Then consider this: The one who finds inner peace is the soul which remembers that it has already attained it in the eyes of God. How much of what you do in life flows from your need to prove that you are capable and have the ability to succeed in this world? What if you knew you had already *made it* in life? How would that shift your perception of people, things and circumstances? How would that dissolve your fear of not measuring up? How would that free you to simply go for it utilizing all the incredible gifts God has woven into your being?

All things pure, excellent, and beautiful, praise worthy and good in this life flow from God's Spirit within you. Stress appears quickly when you resist the flow of God's love and presence within you.

If Jesus asked you "What do you want me to do for you?" How would you answer that question?

#58: Peace: Consistent Sincerity and Reverence for All of Life

Do you want inner peace? Then practice consistent sincerity and reverence for all of life. Having a sensitive heart toward you, everything and everyone creates authenticity in relationships.

A true peace maker in life practices consistent sincerity and reverence for all of life. Practice having reverence for all of life; including your own. Remember that you can only give out to the world around you what you nurture within yourself.

According to Webster, sincerity means: "without deceit, genuine." Reverence means a feeling of deep respect, love and awe. Can you imagine if you made this a daily practice? Remember that love evokes love. Try it, the next time you feel bumped in life, practice returning the "bump" with some expression of love and sincerity, instead of a negative response, and watch how the entire energy surrounding the stressful situation shifts.

#59: Life Is To Love and To Be Loved

Did you know that? All the antics and charades you play out in this life are all fueled by your deepest human desire: to know yourself as loved and to experience loving. In all aspects of your life, your actions are fueled by your desire to see and be seen and to love and be loved. It is in the experience of truly seeing yourself as God sees you that you remember you are loved, profoundly, just as you are.

One of my favorite quotes comes from St. Theresa of Lisieux: *"God sees us for who we are, not for what we do and who we are in His eyes is what we truly desire to be."* When you remember what fuels your soul, you can then align yourself daily with it. The result is inner peace and confidence.

Mother Teresa spoke about this as she referenced her experiences serving the poorest of poor in this world. She said that every human being simply wants to know themselves as loved, as worthy of love and then even in death they have great peace. Understand the flow of love: God . . . Self . . . Neighbor.

"Dear God, thank you for another day of life, to learn how to love better; to experience loving and being loved. Protect me from becoming distracted by those things in life that do not nurture my basic need for inner peace. Grant me the grace to pursue the way of love in all that I do and say in this day."

#60: Move from the King of Your Organs

Did you know that brain cells can be found in your heart? Your heart has the ability to *think*. It can receive and process information. The nervous system within your heart (referred to as the "heart brain") enables it to remember, learn and make functional decisions independent of the brain's cerebral cortex.

Your brain's electromagnetic field goes out two inches from your head. Your heart's electromagnetic field travels out 10 feet from your body in a 360 degree sphere, and it sends out information (frequencies) 24 hours a day. Your emotional state is communicated through your heart's electromagnetic field. The beliefs and images you hold from the past influence your entire life perception and physical well-being. This is why it is so essential for your overall health to replace your negative beliefs with positive ones. For more information on the power of your heart explore The Institute of Heartmath®.

At the end of your day, when you feel burnt out, reflect on how much time you spent *in your head* analyzing, concluding and interpreting versus *your heart* experiencing and feeling. Know that anytime you spend connecting to that which you value most in life you are moving away from your heart, which has been referred to as the head of the body. Replacing the common phrase of "I think" to "I feel" allows you to shift out of your head and into your heart. Peace flows from the heart out into the world. Life is meant to be experienced not defined. Loving God and your neighbor with all of your heart speaks to the truth that God's love flows through the human heart. Do you want peace to return? Then return to your heart. Breathe deeply and connect to the positive experiences in life that move your heart.

You experience and feel life through your heart; you analyze and define it through your head.

#61: Love Exists Outside of Desire

Once again, I reference one of my favorite mentors, Anthony de Mello. True love stands apart from desire in life. When you desire something it is usually linked to the experience of attachment: *"I need this thing, person or outcome in order to be happy."*

The kind of love that God offers you is not based on outcomes. It is patient, kind, good, true and exists outside of the five senses. Desire, however, is confined to the five senses, momentary and limited. A desire in life always leaves you longing for more of that which you desire to possess. This poses a threat that you may not get what you desire, leading you into fear; whereas God's love walks hand-in-hand with contentment. Desire is a craving that continually seeks to be satisfied; whereas love breeds satisfaction and inner calm.

Love or fear? It's your choice. When tempted to fear, say out loud: "I choose love." Words are powerful guides to inner transformation. What causes you to withhold love in your life: from God, yourself and others? Is it a desire or past pain? Explore the ways in which you can connect to love over desire in your life. Again, when you know what you value most in life and nurture that on a daily basis, the doors to loving and being loved are opened up to you.

#62: Choose Love

When I was going through cancer treatment, I would repeat a little mantra: "I choose love and life no matter what surrounds me." Your choice for love no matter what surrounds you will guide you back into peace. Saying, "I choose love" throughout your day can transform your life. I am confident it played a huge part in saving mine.

People helping people is one of the most beautiful opportunities to witness love in action. Look for the opportunity to help another person. Choose love today. Love has no need to own, control or possess. It simply is.

Love transforms the human heart; judgment imprisons it. In your choice for love, it is essential to release all judgments of yourself and others. Look out for that inner critic, you will judge the world around you as you judge yourself. When you embrace God's love for you, leading you into love for yourself, you will then offer that gift to those around you.

> *"It is love alone that brings worth to all things."* —***St. Teresa of Avila***

#63: Dance, Whistle, Sing

As with laughter, when you dance, whistle and sing in life you unleash healing within your body. Everything, from an increased immune system to a decrease in the stress hormone, along with improved cognitive thinking and increased energy, are yours when you laugh, dance, whistle and sing.

Dancing, whistling and singing are all exercises that require you to be present in the moment. God meets you in the present moment, not in the future or in your past. He meets you today, right now. So, anything you can do to keep yourself in the present life in front of your face, do it.

This is why when something is stressing you out, and you ask yourself, "What action can I take *right now*"; you are capable of returning to your place of peace. Action taken in the present moment leads you back into peace, even if that action involves letting go. Anxiety comes when you start to live in the past or future where you cannot take action. Bring yourself to the NOW experience of life.

Next time you feel overwhelmed by life, after you have done your "stressor/action" sheet pick one of your favorite songs and start whistling, humming or singing. Throw in a dance move or two and you will find that inner peace returns. Eckhart Tolle reminds humanity of the truth that no moment of life has ever occurred outside of the present moment.

TO BE? OR NOT TO BE?

Peace of mind and heart occur within the experience of the present moment. You can choose to experience being present to the life in front of your face or not. In your choice lies your peace.

#64: Observe versus React to Life
In order to observe your life you need to be present to your life. You spend most of your time in your head figuring out ways to avoid the fears you have in the future or working through regrets you have from your past. Don't forget the benefits of exploring life through your heart.

When you react to life with a strong negative emotion, you are pulling from your past pictures or holographs in life that are triggered, because of an element in your present encounter that links to your past experience. Often times you will say, "I don't know why I overreacted like that." Remember that the memories stored in the subconscious experience when uploaded by the conscious experience play out as if they are current events. So, the emotion you had at that point on your time line has the same intensity as it did back then. Being the observer of this reactive behavior gives you a little gap of empowerment allowing you the opportunity to shift your perception of the situation; adjust and reframe it into the positive.

Irritations are self-oriented and flow from your need to maintain control in this life. Practice the art of surrender and release as you go through your day.

"God give me eyes to see all the reminders you send my way today to remain present to each moment in life."

#65: Who Do I Say Sent Me?
In the book of Exodus Chapter 3, Moses encounters God in the burning bush where God asks Moses to deliver the Israelites. The part that always gets me is when Moses basically asks God . . . "Sooo . . . who shall I say sent me? Just in case they ask." This is such a human response. When you find yourself stepping into an unfamiliar territory you will often want some backing, as insurance, that you will be accepted or validated. Can you imagine walking into a large group of people who are being oppressed and telling them God sent you to deliver them?

Now, if the CEO of the company sends you with a message on his/her behalf you walk in with an air of confidence in your step. God could have responded to Moses' question with a resume that would have blown anyone out of the water. However, God chose a response which unveiled how He comes to His children: in the present moment. God told Moses to tell the Israelites that, "I AM has sent me to you." Now, can you imagine the silence in the room after that response? "What do you mean I AM sent you? Who the heck is I AM?"

God sends you out every day, moment by moment to bring light and love into this world. You experience God in the present moment. This is why, when you spend time in your mind focusing on the future or the past, you get in a frenzy. The future and past are void of the very presence of God. God is now, in each breath and heartbeat. Don't miss Him.

#66: Begin Again
From the new dawn to the setting of the sun, endless opportunities exist to begin again, learn and grow . . . stay awake!

Seek to nurture your heart in the ways of godliness and love. Part of this experience involves feeling comfortable to begin again, often times several times a day. So, you start out with the intention to choose love and confidence in all that you do. Then, one hour after this intention you find yourself moving against it. Rather than fertilizing your feelings of self-doubt, make the choice to begin again.

You have done this many times in life as you learned new tricks and techniques. For example, when you learned how to walk, you fell many times, yet did not focus on the fall. You stood up as fast as you fell down, beginning again with confidence in your ability to figure it out. Why did you forget that you have the ability to figure anything out by coming up with creative solutions to life's challenges? You did this when you learned how to crawl, walk, talk, run, skip, jump rope and ride a bike.

Remember this experience of beginning again, which has led you to where you are today. Release the self-doubt that has caused you to forget that you are capable of handling any situation in life.

#67: Be Still and Know
Are you seeking guidance in life? Inspiration? Wisdom? Then, practice stillness in life.

Nature resonates with stillness. So, try to get yourself in nature as much as possible, even if it's looking at pictures of nature. Nature reminds you of the stillness that exists within you that is often drowned out by the noise of the world.

Get outside and focus on something in nature for at least three minutes each day. Use as many of your five senses as possible, breathe out all the way and relax as you breathe in deeply. Then, return to your life and notice how your perception shifts from the outside into the inside out. Practice being present to the people you encounter in your day. Play the narrator of your life, if you have too many thought distractions. Narrate what you are doing in the present moment with your inside voice. You will find this brings you into what's happening NOW.

It is in the experience of stillness that the knowing you seek will emerge.

#68: How Do I Do This?

"How do I do this?" I have repeatedly heard this phrase from individuals who are experiencing the pain of loss. "How do I do this?" is a question that as human beings we will face in life, whenever we encounter situations that are unfamiliar to us. Situations will arise when we do not have past experiences to pull from, "the last time this happened this is how I walked through it." Releasing the *do* part of this phrase and simply *be* in the midst of that which is unfolding before you will, in fact, carry you through any and every experience that manifests itself in life.

Last year I had the opportunity to speak at an amazing church in Fiji, I also had the opportunity to see many of their crafts. As I was looking at a wall filled with every imaginable hand held weapon, each hand carved from wood, a voice behind me said, *"Do you like our weapons?"* I turned to find this man with the biggest smile I think I have ever seen. He went on to say, *"Yes, these are beautiful weapons. Did you know we used them when we were cannibals?"* After a long pause gazing into his eyes I replied, *"No, I did not know that. Did you use these weapons?"* He smiled even wider and laughed, *"Not these specific ones, but ones just like these."* He continued to smile as he went on to describe in great detail how each weapon was used.

He then paused and laughed saying, *"Yes, we are not cannibals any more . . . we love God now and eating people and loving God do not go well together."* I spent a lot of time with the Fijians. The people I met were amazing. When I spoke at their church, I was moved to share what I had been witnessing among them the entire time I was there: the endless love, laughter and joy that flowed continuously through each individual that I met. What was the source of this overflow of positive emotions and expressions among them? One of the leaders among the group shared with me after their gathering: *"We believe that everything belongs to God, we surrender all that we are to Him, we release all that we have to God . . . all day long, all night long, and we never run out of joy and love, the laughter comes from our inner joy of knowing how much God loves us . . . that is all."* That is all.

This is an example of people who choose to surrender themselves to God in each moment, because they are present to this experience, there is no *doing* or *striving* necessary to know themselves as loved. It is *reality* for them, and they have made the choice to surrender all that they are to all that God is . . . their joy is complete.

Perhaps the next time you find yourself asking the question, "How do I do this?" you can remind yourself of the power and strength that flows from the experience of giving yourself permission to simply *be* . . . one breath, one heart beat at a time . . . perhaps you will find yourself carried through the storms of life in spite of your self-doubt.

Today, choose to turn everything over to God as each moment unfolds before you . . . no exceptions.

#69: Random Acts of Kindness

Yes, it's true. When you practice random acts of kindness and gratitude on a daily basis you get physiological benefits in the Earth suit: increased immune system; improved cognitive performance; increased energy; lower heart rate; balanced cortisol levels, which result in less internal stress; more likely to live a longer and a more satisfied life; laughter and inner joy, resulting in decreased stress hormones; lower blood pressure and diminished pain.

Wow, that's a lot of benefits! So, how often throughout your day do you practice gratitude and carry out random acts of kindness to those around you, including yourself?

Remember two essential needs of every human being are safety and connection. When you feel connected in life, you feel seen and safe. Remember the line from Avatar? "I SEE you." When you *see* another human being as they are, not as *you* are, you open yourself up to an authentic connection, which leads to positive benefits—including a profound sense of safety.

When you connect yourself to all that is good and beautiful in life, practicing random acts of kindness accomplishes this very quickly, peace returns within your heart. The result will be a shift in your entire perception of events, people and situations as you are seeing them all through the lens of inner connection, gratitude and peace. You will also notice more positive options and solutions available to you in life, as you move from an inner experience of abundance verses lack. As Einstein said, *"The field directly affects the particle."* The particle also affects the field. Your choice to nurture what is good and beautiful in life . . . giving, loving and gratitude . . . will return to you tenfold.

You will begin to remember who you are, that you are created in love, for love, by love, to love: God, yourself and others. An unexplainable sense of well-being begins to fill up what is lacking within you as a result of your past pain and false beliefs. "Oh" you say, "I simply forgot that joy returns quickly when I practice gratitude and acts of kindness." Now, you have the opportunity to remember.

#70: Understanding Omnipresence

One definition of omnipresence is to be present everywhere simultaneously. God is omnipresent. He meets you in the present moment; wherever your present moment happens to be. Your greatest peace always comes when you remain present to the moment of life in front of your face.

The power of God's presence in nature calms the soul/body instantly when you are present to it. Choosing an inspirational verse or saying and repeating it throughout your day creates enough of a mental distraction to keep you present; safe from the fog of the future or regrets from your past.

Want to know peace? Know God. Want to know God? Practice stillness within your day. You will find strength in quietness and trust. Do animals ever fret over whether or not they will have enough grass to eat tomorrow? No, they simply enjoy the grass that is available to them today without any thought of *lack* in the future.

#71: Linger in Life

Do you linger in life or do you rush through your days? Explore the experience of slowing down in your moments. Your to do list often robs you of sacred moments in life that have the ability to draw you back into peace.

Linger in the essential moments in life, the moments that result in a deeper heart connection to God, yourself or others. If you want God pursue godliness. If you want peace, live peacefully. If you want joy, be grateful and pursue laughter. Linger more in the experiences of life without trying to define, own or control it all.

Linger in peaceful moments. Be a channel of peace. Whatever you desire to see, come back to you in life . . . BE THAT. What you desire to see in your life flows directly from your choice to pursue within that which you desire to experience. Love is always a great choice for peace.

#72: Are You Defined By Your List?

Lists are productive in life until you give them the power to define you.

What is on your inner list of requirements to accept yourself just as you are? It's worth sitting down and writing it out. Once you are aware of the power you give your list to define you, you are enabled to adjust your perception.

For example, if your list says: "I will accept myself when I am able to keep up with everything at work and at home," understand that if you don't check off everything that is in line with your definition of "keeping up" then you will experience stress and anxiety. This stress flows from your feelings of inadequacy or self-doubt: "I do not accept and love myself because I did not accomplish everything on my list."

How about this reframe: "Even though I had a huge to do list today and I did not accomplish it all, I am willing to love and accept myself anyway. I am willing to consider that perhaps I had too much on my plate. I choose to be compassionate with myself, and I'm willing to consider that I did the best I could with the time and resources available to me." This takes into consideration physical and emotional aspects that perhaps played a part throughout your day.

Define *you* first as connected to the living God where all things are possible, and you are more than enough, just as you are . . . then go for what you want in life.

REMAIN OPEN TO LOVE

#73: You Always Do That!
As mentioned earlier, Richard Bandler and John Grinder are the founding fathers of NLP (Neuro Linguistic Programming). NLP is basically a study of your objective experiences and what can be calculated from those experiences based on the belief that all behavior has a structure to it.

People bring the same life experiences in, yet in radically different ways. You have created different models and in those models you make the best choices possible for yourself based on the structure of your models. You take in information and act on it through your five senses. You then, use your language to order your thoughts and behavior and communicate; and you *program it all* by organizing and placing meaning on it. This result is the creation of your different models of perceiving life. Here, you use distinctive mechanisms or techniques to process your life models.

"Be careful not to mistake your 'model' of choice for reality," say Bandler and Grinder. They suggest that we all use three mechanisms to do this: generalization, distortion and deletion.

"You always do that!" is a perfect example of a generalization. Perhaps the behavior that you perceive as *always being done* flows from a lens you have created for yourself based on feeling that you are victimized by this behavior. When you were eight you were laughed at and mocked for sharing your feelings. For the rest of your life, if that becomes one of your models, you will reference all moments of laughter in your presence to it and generalize that "any time anyone laughs after I share my feelings, they are mocking me."

> *"We will eliminate judgment of one another when we can understand that all human behavior occurs within the context in which it originated."*
> **—Bandler and Grinder**

#74: You Don't Love Me
According to Bandler and Grinder, deletion is the process by which you selectively pay attention to certain aspects of your experience and exclude others. For example, you have the ability to focus in on one conversation in a very crowded room and block out the other voices. The same holds true for your perception of other people's behaviors. Based on your own models of love you have

the ability to block out other people's behavior completely if it does not fit into your model.

A common block in relationships is overlooking loving expressions (words, gestures, actions), because your model contains generalizations you have made about your own sense of worth, when it comes to loving and being loved. So, you become incapable (when viewing your loved one through your model) of taking in and processing any loving action or word.

To gain an accurate perception of another's words and actions towards you, become aware of the models you have created around the experience of loving and being loved. Do you feel worthy of love? Do you feel capable of loving and being loved? Do you carry feelings of inadequacy around loving?

> *"Deletion reduces the world to proportions which we feel capable of handling." —**Bandler and Grinder***

#75: The Distortion Dilemma

According to Bandler and Grinder, distortion is *". . . the process which allows us to make a shift in our sensory date."* Basically, in order to stay aligned with your models of the world, you are constantly distorting information that does not fit with your perception of the way you see life (relationships, work, success, loss, parenting, etc.).

Even if you are able to identify pieces of information coming into your experience such as supportive actions and words from those around you,

you will distort your perception of them in order to align yourself with your limited model of the world.

According to Bandler and Grinder, we all block ourselves from richer experiences in life because of our limited models. If you have repeatedly experienced rejection in love you will often make the assumption that something is wrong with you, and that you must not be worth loving, because it never works out. This is a generalization that leads to deleting pieces of essential information that are contrary to your belief. Yet they hold within themselves the potential to create a much richer model of love in your life.

Observe yourself as you go through your day and make a note of experiences that perhaps you have deleted, generalized or distorted; valuable pieces of information that have the potential of expanding your perception of yourself and the world.

Remember, as you open yourself up to more options in life, you expand your ability to face challenges with a positive perspective which has a direct effect on the outcomes in life, including how you see yourself and others.

#76: Emotions Block Me from Seeing You
I have a quote from Anthony de Mello next to my computer that says, *"Whenever there is a strong emotion, positive or negative, I cannot see you."*

It's worth observing your behavior in light of this quote. How often in your day is your ability to see another person as they are skewed by your strong emotions; most of which flow from "the writing on your wall."

Understand that most of your conflicts with others flow from your inability to see things and people as they truly are because your emotions disconnect you from being able to consider all options available to you. You spend too much time worrying over the potential reactions of people or your imagined outcomes in different situations.

Did you know that the German translation for worry means to strangle? The Greek translation means to have a divided mind. Whenever you have the strong emotion of worry entering any situation in life, know that you are compromised in your ability to see things as they truly are.

Remain in your castle, connected to God. Explore taking in life from a grounded perception that is based on being anchored in your ability to remain calm and peaceful no matter what surrounds you. Whether you win the lottery or you lose your job, practice remaining grounded within and your inner peace will remain a constant.

#77: I Love You Because You Love Me

Why do you love another person? Is it because they love you in certain ways or provide you with certain benefits as a result of being in relationship with them? This is a challenging question that is worth exploring.

When you love another because of how they love you, then you become vulnerable to pain in love. True love remains a constant no matter what antics surround it. Unfortunately, much of your loving involves a list of requirements that must be fulfilled in order for you to feel safe giving out your gestures of love.

What if God loved you because you loved God? I know personally, I would be living in the energy of lack. Love does not rise and fall depending on how the world responds to it or judges it. Love endures all environments and situations. Even when love seems to have failed, love still prevails.

Love is an inside job first and foremost, and then it flows out to the world. Having difficulties with love? Go within and explore those rooms in your castle that you have locked up because of past pain and self-doubts. Open up all your doors within to the presence of God's love. When you hold tightly to the keys for fear of rejection you will stay stuck in the vacant rooms you guard for fear of more pain. When you surrender yourself over to God's love for you on all levels, you will regain your sight and ability to hear the messages of love that are not based on any outer response of the world around you. God fills your cup first, and then it overflows to those around you without the expectation of return.

As you drop your expectations and assumption of what love needs to look like, you open yourself up to endless opportunities to grow in all the creative ways love will show in your life. God is matchless in His ability to speak your love language.

#78: The Guilt Factor
Much of your actions in relationships and stress flow from past regrets and pain. Make a list of everything you are consciously aware of that you

would like to erase on your timeline. Then go through that list and mark those events or situations that produce a sense of guilt inside of you as you recall them. Using the EFT method described in the bonus chapter, plug in your specific event to this reframe: "Even though I still have this remaining guilt as a result of this situation from my past, I am willing to love and accept myself. I choose to explore letting go of it, even if it is just a small amount today and perhaps more tomorrow. I am willing to practice releasing the guilt."

Guilt will keep you in a state of emotional paralysis in relationships. You respond to guilt and you carry guilt; both distort your ability to see people and yourself as you truly are.

Remember, you are created in love as are those around you. So, when you encounter those who are difficult to love and choose love and forgiveness in spite of it, have the confidence that your choice will evoke more love in your life. Love always evokes more love. Live a life of love and forgiveness for yourself and others and peace will return.

#79: The Jealousy Jungle

Have you ever experienced jealousy? It's as if a crazy spider monkey takes over within you, you can't think or respond with any amount of clarity. Jealousy or envy flow from an ungrateful heart and, if prolonged, have the ability to physiologically affect your body. Proverbs 14:30 says, *"A heart at peace gives life to the body, but envy rots the bones."*

Jealousy acts as a fertilizer to stress in the body. It flows from feelings of lack and inadequacy. When you find yourself imprisoned by the serpent of jealousy you disconnect yourself from creativity and inner inspiration. Basically, in those moments of envy and jealousy you forget the presence of God within you, and you become consumed with the "I'm not good enough just as I am" mentality.

Whenever you choose to stop the craze of comparison, you open yourself up to your God given ability to celebrate your uniqueness and others. Next time you notice that envy knot in your stomach, start to connect to everything you are grateful for in life. This will get you out of your head and back into your heart where love can have its way with you again. Here, you can remember that you are beautifully and wonderfully created in love and for love, lacking nothing for a life of value.

Have full confidence that the unique beauty you bring into this world contains the essential notes needed to create this beautiful symphony of life, as do those around you.

#80: Own, Control and Possess

How much of your day is spent in the pursuit of owning, controlling and possessing things, people, and situations for your own benefit?

Stress explodes in the midst of these three life distractions: the need to own, control and possess. You spend way too much time hunting these false illusions down in life; time that could be spent on expanding your positive perceptions and experiences. This is a vicious cycle that has no end—until you choose to step off. As soon as you get that which you perceive as needing to have a sense of ownership over, you are then consumed by your fear of losing it.

Deathbed wisdom speaks to this: the only thing you own in this life is your ability to choose God, love and your response to situations. The rest of it simply creates a prison in which you frantically try to validate your ability to control events, people and situations in this life.

Practice feeling safe releasing your need for control in order to feel good about yourself. Feel good about yourself as connected to God (love) and then go for what you want. You will notice that a vast expansion of possibilities will open up to you along with a profound sense of peace when you live a life of surrender and trust.

God's love exists beyond all of our perceptions, conclusions and interpretations; it is truly larger than life.

#81: Giving Your Power Away

Figuratively speaking, as soon as you go up to another human being and ask them to define you, you give your power away. You ask others: "Am I capable; worth loving or intelligent and creative?" and then you believe what they say. As soon as you label their response to you as true then you become a slave to it until you release it. "Oh, okay then it must be true, I am capable," you say. Then another human being comes along and says, "You are incapable" and you believe them.

Do you see how exhausting this can become in your life? You rise on fall depending on how the world judges you at the time and the power you give to those judgments to define you. Take back your ability to define yourself in light of God's love for you and you will regain your inner confidence and peace.

Remember, you are not any comment or response from any human being, unless you choose to be.

DO YOU BEND OR BREAK?

The power of remaining flexible leads to the ability to go with the flow. Rigidity leads to potential "breaks" in life that result in stress. When you remain flexible you open yourself up to opportunities for growth and expansion.

#82: The Rainbow in The Midst of the Storm

From my own experience going through two of the top stressors at the same time: divorce and cancer, I found that the rainbows showed up in the midst of the storm. I didn't have to wait until the storm passed to see the beauty that emerged within the challenges before me. Did you know that God does His greatest work at night and in the middle of life's challenges? Fortitude, integrity, patience, empathy, gratitude, forgiveness, endurance, courage and love all have the potential of emerging within you as you walk through the storms of life. These attributes light up the world.

Again, it all comes down to your ability to identify and adjust your perception of any situation. Stress comes in only when you identify a situation as potentially harmful to you (emotionally or physically). When you have a clear perception of what you want in life, you begin to gather the necessary tools to move in that direction. This seems to be the first step toward moving through any storm in life. Create a clear focus of what you want to happen. For me, I would say everyday: "I choose life and love no matter what surrounds me. I choose to see the rainbows in the midst of the storm." As soon as I chose my focus, my body followed as well as my acuity (sharp vision) to recognize all the assets available to move in the direction of my focus. So of course, I started to see all the rainbows (learning opportunities, expressions of love and support, possibilities for expansion personally and professionally).

Again, it's your choice. Remain flexible and have confidence that the most beautiful rainbows show up while it's still raining! Know what you want, then be open to tuning into all aspects that support the direction you are moving in (use your five senses). Remain flexible so you don't break.

Can you imagine if God chose to make inflexible trees? At the first powerful storm, they would all break.

#83: Goals, Deadlines and Appointments

Did you know that these three make up some of the top stressors in the corporate world? Not to mention our family life, right? How often are you rushing, running, striving to make those appointments, deadlines and achieve your personal goals? There is nothing wrong with having goals, wanting to meet your deadlines and showing up on time for your appointments. The stress comes in the planning and organizing of it all.

More often than not, you don't allow enough time to prepare and explore creatively as you work to meet your deadlines. (It's worth rereading the procrastination chapter.) Your deadlines and appointments often times fall in line with your goals in life. To help eliminate the stress, look for ways to allow more time. Set your priorities before you start moving in the direction of meeting your deadlines. Realize you only have so much time in your day and to avoid burnout. It's essential to weave in moments to nurture what you value most in life along with moments to simply *play*. This will end up maximizing the time you spend moving in the direction of your deadlines and goals.

Improved cognitive thinking is one of the physiological benefits of taking time to de-stress your life. You often think, "I just have to work longer hours." Not true. Maximization and efficiency emerge when your mind is clear and focused. These things flow from the moments of play, random acts of kindness, and valuable connections in life . . . along with deep breathing and relaxation techniques.

#84: Something Inside You is Superior to Circumstance

On my refrigerator, I have this quote:

> *All things splendid have been achieved by those who dared to believe that something inside them was superior to circumstance.* —**Bruce Barton**

When I was diagnosed with stage three breast cancer, in the midst of the divorce, I was told I had about a 50 percent chance of survival. Then after 16 chemos, 12 surgeries, six weeks of daily radiation and one year of herceptin infusions I only bumped it up about 15 to a 65 percent chance. I remained in the top groups for a recurrence. I had to do some serious adjusting within.

The quote from Bruce Barton became a part of my daily mantras. If I could truly embrace the belief that something inside of me (God, love, joy) was greater than the circumstance, I could feel peace in the midst of any pain (emotionally or physically).

What circumstance in your life do you feel challenged by? Shift your focus to remembering the One who wove you together, along with the entire Universe, is greater than any circumstance you feel overwhelmed by in life. That power lives within you daily, yet you forget. Today, dare to believe that the strength and love within you is greater than ANY circumstance in life . . . DARE to believe this and watch your world light up.

#85: Complaining IS a Choice

Have you ever complained in life? Of course you have. Have you ever wondered: "Where does complaining come from?" The majority of it actually flows from your feelings of deservedness: "I deserve this to be better, and it's not. So, I'm going to complain about it because I think I deserve more." This is just another serpent in your life that will rot your bones. It is different from feeling worthy in life. Your feelings of worthiness or unworthiness, flow from validating or invalidating experiences in life. When you feel worthy, you feel valued, which happens easily when you remember your connection to God.

Deservedness flows from your EGO and often times is accompanied by anger, which is always fueled by fear. It will often say: "If I don't get this the way I want it then I won't accept myself or those around me." It is accusatory, fault finding and usually leads to complaining in life.

Gratitude is the cure for complaining and a great stress reliever. When you focus on what is working out for you instead of what is not, you shift your entire perception. Then, the acuity to recognize the beauty and wonderment in life returns, lighting up the world. Again, the choice is yours all day long.

#86: The Sky Remains Blue beyond the Clouds

This is a grace from God. To be able to live by faith in the midst of the most challenging moments in life, the dark night of the soul experiences, is a grace. I like Webster's definition of grace: "The love and favor of God towards men."

God's grace appears moment to moment. This is why when you spend time thinking about your future, you worry. Your future does not contain the present gift of grace from God. You want strength and a positive perspective in life? Then remain present to the life in front of your face. Ask God for the ability to embrace the grace of the moment that is constantly available to you. This is a concept that is worth repeating in every chapter simply because it holds such powerful potential to guide you back into peace no matter what surrounds you.

> *When God helps you, it is easy to lift even the world and hold it up like a child's toy.* —**Maria Valtorta, Poem of The Man-God**

However, when we forget that the sky is always blue beyond the clouds,

> *. . . even the weight of a flower is a burden to us.* —**Maria Valtorta**

#87: God's Love is a Constant
Remembering this will help you to bend in life rather than break. God's love is a constant in your life. You just forget because of past pain and false beliefs. It is important to understand that God's love is not defined by the way humans love. So, refrain from projecting your limitations and the limitations of others onto God. In spite of your

feelings of scarcity at times on this journey, the abundance of God's love remains constant.

Too often as human beings using only about five percent of our brain capacity, we will limit our perceptions of God based on our experiences with other humans.

Have you ever had a negative encounter with someone who claimed to know God, and you then misplaced your disappointment and frustrations from their actions onto God? Perhaps you even disengaged from your own pursuit of knowing and loving God as a result of another's negative witness. God's love is very different from how you love as a human being. This is why it is so essential to connect to God in our experience of loving in this world. Our love is limited. God's love is limitless. Our love will often contain criteria and is conditional, God's love simply is and exists beyond reason, conditions and requirements . . . it is unconditional and constant.

A verse from Isaiah 50:15–16 sums this chapter up beautifully: *"Can a mother forget the baby at her breast and have no compassion on the child she has borne? Though she may forget, I will not forget you! See, I have engraved you on the palms of my hands; your walls are ever before me."* It is grounding and peaceful to remember that you are remembered constantly by love itself.

#88: Avoid the Deer in the Headlights

The "deer in the headlights" response to life is a direct result of a disruption in your body's energy system. When you experience anything in life that you define as a threat to your safety (emotionally or physically), the flow of energy through your brain and body actually freezes. You get the wide eyes, increased blood pressure and increased stress hormone that comes along with it.

What events, situations or responses in your life trigger a "deer in the headlights" response? When you keep your energy moving in life through remaining flexible, identifying and adjusting your perceptions and physically tap on major meridians (energy points, see attached chapter at the end of the book) you are less likely to experience the *freeze*. When your energy is moving and something *bumps* you in life you are more capable of shifting on the spot to a perception that leads you back to peace.

Another quick tip to help release the freeze: breathe out all the way as far as you can, then relax and allow yourself to naturally breathe in deeply, tune into a moment in time when this was not a problem for you. Roll your eyes around in one direction and then the other way. Tap on your thymus, which is two inches below the U-shaped dip at the base of your neck, and repeat for one minute: "I have faith and confidence in God, my future is secure; I am secure."

#89: Just Let It Go!

"Just let it go" . . . a lot easier said than done eh? How can I let this go? Who will I be if I let it go? I've identified with this for so long I don't feel safe embracing a new perception of me. Will I really be okay if I just "let go and let God?" Can I trust in that experience? Will I be able to handle it? What exactly does that look like? Who will I be if I release that perception, that outlook, that pain?

Again, when you give anything in life the permission to define you, you gravitate toward it, you attract more of it, and you feel safe connecting to it. So, you will actually cling to it over a healthier perception of self simply because you know yourself within it. Remember, human beings gravitate toward that which is familiar, even if the familiar is unhealthy and, often times, unsafe.

So, how do you "Let go and Let God?" How do you give yourself permission to embrace a new perception, a new direction, a new connection with you, with God, with the world when you have identified with this perception of *you* your entire life? Understanding the power you have given away to things, people and circumstances is the first step of empowerment and into a new perception of self. It is a journey back to you before the pain and false beliefs kicked in. Take some time to retrieve those parts of you that you farmed out to others throughout your life time. Acceptance and forgiveness are two essential ingredients when letting anything go in this life.

Choose to love no matter what: "Even though this happened, I choose love and release for the purpose of remembering who I am apart from my pain." Any time you return to love, self-acceptance and forgiveness, you return and connect to the very essence of God, the authentic self apart from any attachment to pain and the power you have given to it to define who you are. Explore beginning your day with: "I choose to take back my power to define me, in, with and through the experience of God's Love."

#90: Do You Fight, Fly, or Freeze?
The scientific world is coming forth with study after study that reveals the truth of this statement: A heart at peace leads to life.

It is worth repeating what *exactly* happens in a body exposed to continual stress.

- Cortisol levels go up (the stress hormone)
- Blood pressure and cholesterol production increase
- Body acidity increases
- Major organs become vitamin and mineral depleted, due to your body's attempt to alkalize your blood
- Allergies develop
- Immune system is compromised
- Gut flora is reduced
- Insomnia
- Loss of self-esteem
- Post traumas emerge
- Hyper-vigilance increases, along with panic attacks and OCD behaviors

Additionally,

- You make unhealthy choices, in an attempt to comfort yourself in the midst of continual stress: drugs, medications, alcohol, sugar, all of which are quick fixes.

- Complex thinking and your ability to problem solve are severely compromised, and
- You may be able to take in information faster, but your ability to process it all is stunted.

Remember the definition of stress? Stress is a signal within your body giving you the opportunity to identify and adjust your perception of a situation and your behavior. You are not a victim here in life, unless you choose to be. Fighting, fleeing or freezing are common responses to stressful situations. You can stay and fight, or resist, what is, or you can shift your perception and begin to seek creative solutions and options. You can run away from what you perceive to be a stressful situation, or you can take action and seek resolution. You can freeze or remain emotionally paralyzed. Alternatively, you can use the techniques you learned in #88 to unfreeze and move on in life.

You can't always choose what unfolds before you in this life; however, you always have the ability to choose how you respond.

IS YOUR ANCHOR SINKING YOUR BOAT?

As you go through life you begin to gather pieces from your experiences that end up creating "your anchor" in life. The problem comes when those pieces do not allow you to leave the harbor, and you remain stuck. What you think is the source of your happiness is, often times, the very aspect that has the potential to sink your boat. A healthy anchor is one that travels with you as you explore the ocean of life, allowing you moments of retreat from tumultuous waters. What makes up your anchor in life?

#91: Expectations and Assumptions Sink Your Boat
Do you want a boat that floats in life? Then release your expectations and assumptions of how you think things should turn out. Yes, flexibility is a huge part in this practice. Whenever you enter a

situation with set expectations or assumptions, you set yourself up for stress. Planning has value until you try to control the outcome.

Plan and release: Do your best in life and surrender the outcome. When you expect and assume in relationships you are pulling from life that has not even occurred, you are referencing an imagined situation. You accomplish your goals in life when you do all you can do in the present moment. Creativity and inspiration flow in presence. This is not to negate the value in positive thinking, when you visualize a positive outcome; however, your boat will begin to sink if you expect things to unfold a certain way. This is why the practice of surrender is so valuable in life. Let go and let God has become a beneficial statement over time, yet how often is it practiced?

Do your best and realize that you are always doing your best with the resources you have available to you in that moment (emotionally and physically). Delete the habit of expecting and assuming (ask for clarity). Then surrender the work of your hands to God who is able to produce roses in the midst of thorns, blooms in the middle of the desert and rainbows amidst the storms.

#92: Curiosity and Fascination Float Your Boat

Being committed to curiosity and fascination towards all of life has the potential to transform your entire horizon. You used to move from this energy when you were little. Curious about everything from a small roly-poly to a cucumber; you lived in the wonderment of the present moment.

Is Your Anchor Sinking Your Boat?

You laughed deeply, cried deeply moved and spoke with expression and enthusiasm; especially around your new discoveries in life. What happened? You forgot how to explore, create and live in awe and wonder. The world didn't become boring all of a sudden. You merely lost your vision and ability to hear and experience life and all of its abundance.

Practice being a curious and fascinated human being. Ask how and what questions to gain more information verses why questions that keep you stuck in life. Abandon your need to know why things happen as they do. Next time someone rocks your boat, become curious: "Hmmm, that's interesting, I wonder what is behind that expression or response." When you are intrigued and fascinated you are empowered on all levels to choose your response to any situation with cognitive clarity.

Children learn very quickly because of their spirit of curiosity. When you assume you close doors to creative thinking and solutions, when you are curious you open all doors, all possibilities, a true "thinking out of the box" experience.

#93: Go With the Flow
Nothing unleashes the flow of life faster than the still experience of God within. This simple truth resonates throughout all of nature. As I sat this summer at the foot of this grand waterfall, I observed the effortless connection between stillness and flow. The trees in their silent, grounded nature cradled the majestic flow of water between them. I am awe struck once again at how perfectly

God has woven into nature simple truths that if embraced and lived out have an unlimited potential for unleashing life's connection and inner peace.

Today take a few moments to observe something beautiful in nature. You may want to explore the following question: "What is hidden here that I may not see because I am giving into the blinding experience of living in the noise of my head versus the stillness of my heart?"

Reflection: Notice how worry, doubt and fear are void of all stillness and calm; whereas love and gratitude resonate and flow abundantly with it. Whatever your choice of focus is in life grows bigger.

What happens to a pond without any flow? It becomes stagnant. What happens to the body when the flow of breath, heartbeat and blood stop, when the flow of the spirit within moves on? It becomes stiff. Flow is essential for life to flourish. Practice moving with the flow of life rather than resisting it. Your ability to ride the waves of life is found in your ability to go with the flow.

#94: Avoid Tunnel Vision: Expand Your Options

The next time you find yourself in a stressful situation, shift your focus to all available options as quickly as possible. Identifying more options allows you to expand and enrich your programs of response to life. This is why wording is so essential when you find yourself feeling stuck in life. Simply adding on a few words can shift your entire perception of your abilities in challenging situations. You always have options to expand your language to include statements that resonate with possibilities. For example, here are two popular statements: "I can't do that!" and "I don't know how." You can feel the stagnation. Simply adding a few words can open the door to possible solutions: "I can't do that yet, but I believe I am capable of learning how" and "I don't know how to do that, yet I believe I can figure it out with the right resources."

Expand your options in your language and your behavior. Even though you are familiar with certain responses in life and defend those responses with, "I always do it this way" explore different ways of going about life. Explore different ways of moving from point A to point B (you did this all the time as a child). Explore different ways of speaking and connecting with people in life along with different ways to express your inner inspirations. The more you explore, the more you expand your options and possible creative solutions. The more you nurture spontaneity and creativity, the lighter life will become.

#95: Practice Integrity
Want life, prosperity and honor? Pursue godliness, integrity and love in all you do. A person of integrity keeps careful watch over the words that flow out of their mouth. Whatever you put into the world comes back to you. Use your delete key when it comes to gossiping.

Do you want to live on God's *holy hill*? Slander no one . . . including yourself. Keep vigilant watch on the inner critic, it serves no one on earth.

Having an integrous spirit involves sincerity: having an authentic concern for those around you and living your life without deceit. This is one of the essential attributes in life that holds within itself the ability to light up the world.

Remember, God does His greatest work in the eye of the storm. Integrity, fortitude, vigilance, empathy, patience and love are all developed and strengthened during the trials of life. So, do not fear those dark nights of life, for within them, you find the greatest potential for learning and growth.

#96: EGO Sinks: Vulnerability Floats

Many spiritual teachers have referenced the antics of the EGO and its ability to distract you from God. Your EGO or "Edging God Out" needs to have you as the center of your life: your needs, wants, desires, position and esteem, all of it, right smack in the middle of your life. Basically saying, "What's mine is mine and what's yours is mine." It involves expectations and assumptions along with deservedness. The EGO is like a spoiled child; the more you give it, feed it, nurture it and protect it, the more it wants. It is never satisfied and is addicted to the drug of approval. It exists in fear and pride.

The EGO feeds off of past and future fears, doubts and worries: "What will other people think?" It can't exist when you make the choice to be acutely aware and present to the life in front of your face. Can you recognize the antics of the EGO within you? Know that your boat will sink if you live by the EGO's demands: "I need to be seen, heard, esteemed, acknowledged and praised in order to feel good about myself."

Vulnerability, on the other hand, is birthed through the trials in life and exists in presence, humility and love. Vulnerability evokes love instantly within the human heart. When you allow yourself to be vulnerable, on any level in life, you open yourself up to instant connection with humanity. Think about it, the moments in life when you are deeply moved by the suffering of an animal or human being connects you to their vulnerability. Instinctively, love is your response.

When I walked around bald throughout my chemo treatments, I witnessed this on a daily basis. The outpouring of random acts of kindness, due to my willingness to be vulnerable, was profound. The expressions of love through gifts, cards, coffee, meals, words of affirmation, smiles, embraces all left me in awe at the power vulnerability possesses to unleash love in the heart. I often reflect on this when I contemplate the silent, holy night when God entering the world as a baby—the ultimate expression of vulnerability and love.

> *"Dear God, protect me from compliments*
> *and complaints that I may remain*
> *steadfast in my ability to hear*
> *your voice over worldly static."*

#97: Look for the Lighthouse

Ask, seek and knock are three actions in life that can result in inner guidance. Now, it's important to reference a little wisdom here from the book of James Chapter 4:1-3. In these few versus, James calls us out on our motives in life. He says that the conflicts we experience with each other come from the battle with our own desires within: *"You want something but don't get it. You quarrel and fight. You do not have, because you do not ask God. When you ask, you do not receive, because you ask with wrong motives, that you may spend what you get on your pleasures."*

When you seek guidance in life, believe that it will appear. The way to get where you feel called to go already exists, you simply need to tune into it. Remain anchored in integrity when seeking your lighthouse in life. Watch for the antics of your EGO that feeds off of motives stooped in self-indulgence. Practice humility. Reflect on how moved you are to assist the humble in life. The smaller you are, the more room there is for God to be HUGE through you. Seek those things in life that exists beyond the five senses: charity, faith and love and you will receive the essential ingredients needed to lead you back to inner peace.

Look for the lighthouse within you. You are never lost; you simply forget who you are in the midst of life's pain. Whatever you forget, you have the ability to remember.

#98: Love People, Not Things

If your anchor is made up of things, your boat will sink. If it's made up of loving God, your neighbor and you, it will float.

When I was 16, I read every book available by Leo F. Buscaglia, Ph.D. otherwise known as the "love doctor" or "hug doctor." I still reference a quote of his daily: *"People before Things."* Remember, stress will appear when you forget to align yourself with what you value most in this life.

If you are a type "A" personality, then you are familiar with the speed boat approach to life. All too often, people get overlooked as you jet past towards your destination. I know because I was a type A, BC (before cancer). Facing my own death led me into the experience of lingering more in what I value most in the essentials of life.

How many times do you bypass the opportunity to create a meaningful connection with a human being because you are racing through life? Love people, not things. Don't wait until you find yourself on your deathbed to get this one. I assure you, you only remember the people and the love you shared. All things pass away except love.

#99: Don't Want to Sink? Learn How to Swim

As I was sitting across from my counselor, weeping over the loss of my marriage, my hair and my breasts I said: *"I feel like a helpless kitten drowning in the ocean, and I can barely catch my breath."* To which he brilliantly responded, *"How about choosing to be a dolphin that has the ability to swim through it all?"*

How many times have you felt like a helpless kitten in the ocean of life? Have you forgotten that you have the ability to learn how to swim even in the midst of the great white sharks in life? By the way, dolphins have been known to take out sharks.

Your ability to overcome life's challenges and return to inner peace lies in your choice of perception concerning those challenges. Are you a kitten or a dolphin? The choice is yours on all levels. Remember that life is a process involving discovery, learning and growth, not any single event.

You are a drop of life in God's powerful ocean of endless possibilities.

GETTING YOUR ENERGY BEHIND THE SHIFT

The following information is taken from my Award Winning International Best Selling Book: *5 Minutes to Stress Relief, How to Release Worry, Doubt and Fear,* Published by Career Press/New Page Books, This book contains quick and easy stress relief techniques, most of which can be applied under five minutes.

Simple overview of EFT, Healing at Your Fingertips

EFT is not connected to any new age philosophy, spiritual or religious practice. It is simply a mechanical technique similar to physical therapy that helps the body reconnect after an experience of disconnect (energy "freeze") due to emotional blocks and pain. Similar to the benefits of using an EEG and an EKG to monitor energy connections in our brain and heart, EFT monitors our inner energy connections that become disrupted because of emotional pain and false beliefs and offers a way to reconnect within.

Negative emotions cause a disruption in your body's flow at the meridian centers or energy points. Your body then becomes unbalanced, which results in both physical and emotional stress.

Basically, EFT helps to rewire your energetic system that is in a "frozen" state due to the emotional or physical event.

Imagine a television set that is experiencing static. It is in a frozen state because there is some kind of confusion in its wiring or connection. As soon as the rewiring or reconnecting takes place, the clarity of the picture returns.

As soon as you restore balance to your system using this tapping technique, you return to a state of balance within. Therefore, you are no longer upset when faced with the same situation that upset you earlier. I believe it is a beautiful gift from God in that it works with how you are woven together, how your body responds to the environment around you. It should be included in a "How to be a Human Being without all the Stress" handbook. Imagine how helpful that would have been to get after you entered the world.

Consider what happens when people have heart attacks. In an attempt to save a life, an electric current is sent through the body to start the heart.

Getting Your Energy Behind the Shift

Surely, at one point you have experienced getting a shock after walking across the carpet with fuzzy socks? I used to have "shock wars" with my brothers and sister growing up. Why is this possible? It is because of the energy that flows through your body.

There is an electrical circuit that runs through your body and sends messages to your brain controlling all of your functions, both emotional and physical. These centers are found in different places along the electrical circuit of your body and are called meridians.

As you tune into your distressing event, memory, or physical pain (being as specific as possible), while tapping with your fingertips on the different energy points (meridians), you are able to collapse the negative charge that you hold around the physical or emotional pain.

The following meridian points are used in EFT because they are near to the surface of the body and are easier to access:

You begin EFT with a setup statement: stating the event that is stressing you out. You repeat your setup statement **three times**.

- Your set statement is the sentence you start out with that describes with ruthless honesty what you feel and your distressing event. Avoid global statements like, "Even though I'm stressed out," or "Even though I have low self-esteem." The more specific you can be the better the results. Here are too example setup statements: "Even though I'm really ticked off that my boss told me today that I was incompetent, I am willing to love and accept myself just as I am." Or "Even though I have a huge headache that is throbbing behind my eyes, I am willing to love and accept myself anyway."

- Say your setup statement (Even though this happened . . . I am willing to love and accept myself just as I am.) three times while tapping the side of your hand (karate chop point) or rubbing the *sore spots* located two inches down from the U-shaped dip in your neck and three inches over on each side.

- Before you start tapping check in with your emotional or physical pain and rate it on a scale from 1–10.

- Be as specific as you can with your wording.

- Tune in emotionally to the issue and connect with your emotional response as much as possible.

- Use visualization to imagine yourself in the situation that caused you the anxiety or focus on your physical pain.

- Once you are tuned into your issue you begin tapping on the outer soft side of your hand (the karate chop point) or rub the sore spots: there are two spots located to the left and right, 3 inches down and 3 inches over from the dip in your clavicle, either one is effective.

Getting Your Energy Behind the Shift

- Tap on the issue at hand as soon as possible, the quicker you can get your energy moving around the "ZZZZT" disconnect in your body the better.

- After repeating your "setup" statement three times, you are ready to move through a sequence of points while stating a reminder phrase that links you to your setup statement.

- Using the example mentioned above "Even though I have this huge headache, I am willing to love and accept myself anyway" take a one or two word reminder phrase like "this headache" and using your fingertips lightly tap 5–7 times on the following points as you say your reminder phrase one time at each point.

The sequence of EFT points to tap on after the setup:

- The beginning of the eyebrows, just above and to one side of the nose

- The outside of your eye socket bone, between your eyes and your temples

- Under your eyes on the top of the cheekbone about 1 inch below your pupil

- Under your nose, between your upper lip and the bottom of your nose

- Half way between your chin and the bottom of your lower lip

- One inch down and one inch over from the bottom of the U-shape dip on your collarbone at the base of your throat
- Under your arm. Along the bra strap line for a woman. Use your four fingers to tap on this point under the arm.
- The liver point. It is located about one inch down from the nipple for men and right under the breast for a woman.
- The outside edge of your thumb at a point right next to the thumbnail
- The outside edge of your index finger at the nail (facing your thumb)
- The side of your middle finger at the point by the nail (the side closest to your thumb)
- The inside of the baby finger (side closest to your thumb)
- Added point: the top of the head
- End with tapping on the karate chop point on the soft side of your hand.
- I will often leave out the finger points when I tap and get the same results. I add them if I feel stuck.

After you have said your setup statement three times and tapped a round of the sequence point while stating the reminder phrase, check to see how high you pain is (emotional or physical) on the scale from 1–10. Sometimes, it will get higher before it drops. Keep on tapping the sequence of points while saying, ". . . this remaining _____ (insert your reminder phrase)." Keep checking in and tapping until you reach 0.

Don't stress out about memorizing these points. Take your time learn a few each day, and soon you will be tapping in your sleep.

Before you begin to tap, it's helpful to rate your stressful situation or physical pain on a scale from 1–10. Then, tap for a while and try to tune back into your issue to see if it drops down on the scale. If you keep tapping until you get down to a 0 it is unlikely that specific aspect of your painful memory or event will return.

We all have table top issues like low self-esteem and phobias such as fear of speaking in public. Each of these issues can have many aspects. For example, you may experience claustrophobia. That experience, in and of itself, can contain many aspects connected to a painful memory. Perhaps you accidentally locked yourself in a closet and could not get out as a child. You felt trapped, unheard and overlooked. You couldn't breathe and felt powerless.

Each of the above aspects associated with the trauma of being locked in a closet makes up the fear of closed spaces for you and yet each one must be dealt with specifically. Tap on all of them. "Even though I felt trapped in that closet and I couldn't get out, I am willing to love and accept myself anyway." "Even though I couldn't breathe and I thought I was going to die, I am willing to love and accept myself." Each aspect must be released (tapped on until you reach 0) in order for the table to fall. However, many times your aspects are linked together. So, when you collapse one you collapse them all, and you suddenly feel lighter. Feelings like, "Hey, it's no big deal! Why did that upset me so much?" or "I'm over it!" replace the anxiety instantly.

EFT is a very forgiving technique. You don't have to get it all down perfectly for it to still work. As soon as you recognize that "ZZZZT" disconnect in your body due to a physical or emotional pain, start tapping.

Explore more insights, quick stress relief tips and personal excellence and wellness resources at: www.laurenemiller.com.

About the Author

Lauren E Miller, M.Ed, MSC, ICF-PCC

As a stress relief expert, award winning author, motivational speaker, HRD trainer, Edge God In podcast host, and certified executive and life coach, Lauren facilitates fun process driven programs with guidance, support and accountability creating positive sustainable behavioral change in business and personal life.

Lauren has worked in youth and adult ministries for over 30 years. Through God's mercy, grace and strength, she uses her experience simultaneously conquering two of life's top stressors: cancer and divorce to help others destress and successfully move through challenges.

Happily, remarried and gratefully enjoying life in Colorado with a loving husband, three grown children and two grandchildren, Lauren is often found in the kitchen dancing to her favorite worship music or rolling around on the floor with her two dogs.

Lauren holds a Masters in Adult Education with a Certification in Human Resources Development | Advanced Neuro-Linguistic Programming (NLP) Basic & Master Certification | Faculty Shift Leadership Training | Master Sherpa Executive Coach (MSC) and ICF Certification PCC | 2nd degree blackbelt World Tae Kwon Do

She has authored 9 books, 3 of which are Award Winning:

- Hearing His Whisper . . . with every storm Jesus comes too
- 99 Things You Want To Know Before Stressing Out!
- Stop Letting the World Be the Boss of You! 25 Solutions to Refresh Your Identity in Christ

Lauren's Mission Statement: Champion Human Potential in Christ

Equip people and teams globally with mindset skills and sustainable behavioral shifts to de-stress their lives, regain inner clarity of purpose and step into personal and professional fulfillment.

Edge God In Podcast: http://EdgeGodIn.com

EmotionalIntelligenceinChrist.com

http://LaurenEMiller.com

If you've found this book helpful, please share and leave your testimonial review on your favorite bookstore's website.

NOTHING has the POWER to DEFINE YOU unless you give it away.
—Lauren E Miller

LIGHTEN UP, LET GO, and *LIVE!*

EdgeGodIn.com
LaurenEMiller.com

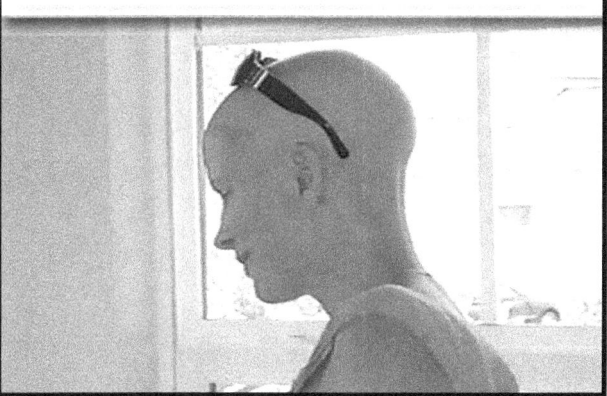

www.ingramcontent.com/pod-product-compliance
Lightning Source LLC
Chambersburg PA
CBHW070428010526
44118CB00014B/1957